10 GRANNY SQUARES **30 BAGS**

Quarto is the authority on a wide range of topics.

Quarto educates, entertains and enriches the lives of
our readers—enthusiasts and lovers of hands-on living.

www.QuartoKnows.com

First published in the United States of America by
Creative Publishing international, an imprint of
Quarto Publishing Group USA Inc.
400 First Avenue North, Suite 400
Minneapolis, MN 55401
1-800-328-3895
QuartoKnows.com
Visit our blogs at QuartoKnows.com

ISBN: 978-1-58923-894-7

Digital edition published in 2016
eISBN: 978-1-62788-715-1

10 9 8 7 6 5 4 3 2 1

Library of Congress Cataloging-in-Publication Data available

Technical Editor: Karen Manthey
Copy Editor: Karen Levy
Design: Laura Shaw Design, Inc.
Illustrations: Karen Manthey
Photographs: Glenn Scott Photography

Printed in China

10 GRANNY SQUARES
30 BAGS

Purses, Totes, Pouches, and Carriers from Favorite Crochet Motifs

Creative Publishing international

DEDICATION

*To my wonderful family,
you fill my life with joy.*

ACKNOWLEDGMENTS

I have said it many times: it takes a tremendous effort on behalf of many people to get a book from the initial idea to completion, and this book was no exception. It was not only a challenging one to do but also lots of fun.

I would like to thank Lion Brand Yarn Company, Berroco, Cascade Yarns, Blue Heron Yarns, Coats and Clark, Hampden Hills Alpacas, Louet Yarns, Lucci Yarns, Tahki/Stacy Charles Yarns, and Universal Yarns for donating all the yarn used in completing these bags. Without their support, my job would be much more difficult.

A huge thank-you to Nancy Smith, Paula Alexander, Jeannine Buehler, Theresa DeLaBarrera, Grace Gardiner-Aquila, Cathie Nolan, Deb Seda-Testut, Dee Stanziano, and Sharon Valencia, the small army of crocheters, who helped me in making all the samples.

Thank you to Karen Manthey, technical editor and diagram creator extraordinaire.

Last, but never least, thank you to Linda Neubauer, my editor, my friend, for guiding me through these many books, and for encouraging me to stretch my mind to embrace new technology. It's a joy working with you.

CONTENTS

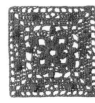

INTRODUCTION

Anyone who knows me knows that I love granny squares. Granny has been very good to me, as this will be my fourth book on granny squares. After *The Granny Square Book*, *Granny Square Flowers*, and *10 Granny Squares 30 Blankets*, you may be asking, "How now, Granny?" *10 Granny Squares 30 Bags* is the newest granny book, and I had such fun coming up with thirty more creative ways to use the beloved crochet motif.

I have created every size and shape bag, from tiny amulet bags to large oversized totes, evening bags, beach bags, backpacks, tablet covers, and more.

A wide range of yarns and fibers have been used for the bags, which demonstrates how wonderfully versatile the granny square can be. For every bag, the specific brands and colors are listed in case you want to make your bag exactly like mine. I have used a lot of different yarns to create really interesting looks. I almost always use a hook smaller than the yarn usually calls for, so that the fabric will be slightly denser, sturdier, and more appropriate for a bag.

Getting the exact gauge is not absolutely necessary for a bag, and you can change yarn weight and hooks to create your own look, just be aware that the finished size of each bag will be different if you make this change and you may also require different amounts of yarn than specified.

One problem with crocheted bags is that they can lose their shape quickly. I almost always line my bags to give them shape, and I give you several different methods for lining. I like to add special touches, like covered snaps or zippers, or embellishing with floral motifs, tassels, or beads. Instructions for all these methods are included.

I hope that you enjoy this book and have fun adding your own special touches to make each bag your own.

Margaret

FLOWER BUDS

Skill Level: Intermediate

Made with 4 colors: A, B, C, and D.

With A, make an adjustable ring.

RND 1: Ch 1, 8 sc in ring, join with a Sl st in first sc, tighten ring. (8 sc)

RND 2: Ch 1, 2 sc in each sc around, join with a Sl st in first sc. (16 sc)

RND 3: Ch 4 (counts as dc, ch 1), (dc, ch 1) in each sc around. Fasten off A. (16 dc; 16 ch-1 sps)

RND 4: With RS facing, join B with a Sl st in any ch-1 sp, ch 3 (counts as dc here and throughout), dc in same sp, 2 dc in each of next 2 ch-1 sps, *(3 dc, ch 3, 3 dc) in next ch-1 sp (corner)**, 2 dc in each of next 3 ch-1 sps, rep from * around, ending last rep at **, join with a Sl st in top of beg ch-3. Fasten off B.

RND 5: With RS facing, join C with a Sl st in any corner ch-3 sp, ch 1, *(3 sc, ch 3, 3 sc) in corner ch-3 sp, *sc in each of the next 5 dc, sk next dc, (sc, ch 8) 3 times in the sp before next dc, sk next dc, sc in each of the next 5 dc, rep from * around, join with a Sl st in first sc. Fasten off C. (12 ch-8 loops; 4 corner ch-3 sps)

RND 6: With RS facing, join D with a Sl st in any corner ch-3 sp, ch 1, *(2 sc, ch 2, 2 sc) in corner ch-3 sp, sc in each of the next 8 sc, ch 1, sk next 3 ch-8 loops, sc in each of the next 8 sc, rep from * around, join with a Sl st in first sc.

RND 7: Ch 1, sc in first st, sk next sc, *(sc, ch 2, sc) in next corner ch-2 sp, sk next sc, sc in each of the next 6 sc, sc in right-hand ch-8 loop and next sc of current rnd, sc in each of next 2 sc, sc in next ch-1 sp, sk center ch-8 loop, sc in each of next 2 sc, sc in left-hand ch-8 loop and next sc in current rnd, sc in each of the next 6 sc, sk next sc, rep from * around, omitting last sc, join with a Sl st in first sc.

RND 8: Ch 1, sc in first sc, sk next sc, *(sc, ch 2, sc) in next corner ch-2 sp, sk next sc, sc in each of the next 9 sc, 6 dc in center ch-8 loop and next sc in current rnd (flower bud made), sc in each of the next 9 sc, sk next sc, rep from * around, omitting last sc, join with a Sl st in first sc. Fasten off D.

RND 9: With RS facing, join B with a Sl st in any corner ch-2 sp, ch 1, *(sc, ch 2, sc) in corner ch-2 sp, sk next sc, sc in each of next 9 sc, ch 1, sk next 6 dc, sc in each of the next 9 sc, sk next sc, rep from * around, join with a Sl st in first sc. Fasten off B.

RND 10: With RS facing, join A with a Sl st in any corner ch-2 sp, ch 1, *(sc, ch 2, sc) in corner ch-2 sp, sk next sc, sc in each of the next 9 sc, sc in next ch-1 sp, sc in each of the next 9 sc, sk next sc, rep from * around, join with a Sl st in first sc. Fasten off.

beach tote

Roomy and colorful, this tote is perfect for carrying everything needed for a day at the beach. Its cheerful citrus colors are reminiscent of a slice of cool watermelon on a bright, sunny day, and the starfish and sand dollars add pops of color and texture to the tote's beachy appeal.

BAG 1

Yarn: [3]

Lion Brand Modern Baby, 50% acrylic, 50% nylon, 173 yd (158 m), 2.6 oz (75 g): 2 skeins each of #194 Chartreuse (A) and #113 Red (B), 1 skein each of #133 Orange (C), #098 White (D), and #130 Green (E)

Hook: F-5 (3.75 mm)

Notions: ¾ yd (0.7 m) of lining fabric, 1½" x 44" (3.8 x 110 cm) strip of interfacing for Gusset (optional), 1½ yd (1.4 m) of drapery cord for Handle

Gauge: Each square = 6" x 6" (15 x 15 cm); 16 sts = 4" (10 cm); 8 rows dc = 4" (10 cm); 18 rows sc = 4" (10 cm)

Finished Size: 19½" wide x 13½" deep (49.5 x 34.5 cm), including gussets

Skill Level: Experienced

SQUARES

Make 6 Flower Bud Squares (page 7) using A for Rnds 1, 2, and 3; D for Rnds 4 and 9; E for Rnd 5; C for Rnds 6, 7, and 8; amd B for Rnd 10. Fasten off, leaving a sewing length.

FRONT/BACK (MAKE 2)

With B, sew 3 squares together into a strip.

TOP STRIPE

ROW 1: With RS facing, join A with a Sl st in top right-hand corner ch-2 sp of Front/Back, ch 1, *sc in each sc across square, sc in corner ch-2 sp**, sk seam, sc in next corner ch-2 sp, rep from * across, ending last rep at **, turn. (69 sc)

ROWS 2–4: Ch 1, sc in each sc across, turn.

ROW 5: Ch 1, sc in first sc, 2 sc in next sc, sc in each sc across to last 2 sc, 2 sc in next sc, sc in last sc, turn. (71 sc)

ROWS 6–8: Ch 1, sc in each sc across, turn.

ROW 9: Rep Row 5. (73 sc)

ROWS 10–12: Ch 1, sc in each sc across, turn.

ROW 13: Rep Row 5. (75 sc)

ROWS 14–18: Ch 1, sc in each sc across, turn.

Fasten off A.

BOTTOM STRIPE

ROW 1: With RS facing and squares on top, join B with Sl st in top right-hand corner ch-2 sp of Front/Back, ch 1, *sc in each sc across square, sc in corner ch-2 sp**, sk seam st, sc in next corner ch-2 sp, rep from * across, ending last rep at **, turn. (69 sc)

ROWS 2–4: Ch 1, sc in each sc across, turn.

ROW 5: Ch 1, sc in first sc, sc2tog over next 2 sts, sc in each sc across to last 3 sc, sc2tog over next 2 sts, sc in last sc, turn. (67 sc)

ROWS 6–8: Ch 1, sc in each st across, turn.

ROW 9: Rep Row 5. (65 sc)

ROWS 10–12: Ch 1, sc in each st across, turn.

ROW 13: Rep Row 5. (63 sc)

ROWS 14–18: Ch 1, sc in each st across, turn.

Fasten off B.

(continued)

GUSSET

With A, ch 10.

ROW 1: Dc in 4th ch from hook, dc each ch across, turn. (8 dc)

ROWS 2–8: Ch 3 (counts as dc), sk first st, dc in each dc across, complete last st with B, fasten off A.

ROWS 9–81: With B, rep Row 2, change to A, fasten off B.

ROWS 82–89: With A, rep Row 2.

EDGING

RND 1: With B, ch 1, *sc in each of next 8 dc, ch 1, rotate, working across long side of Gusset, sc in same sp as last sc, sc in same row-end dc, matching colors to stripes, 2 sc in each row-end dc in A, change to B, 2 sc in each row-end dc in B, change to A, 2 sc in each row-end dc in A, ch 1, rep from * once, ch 1, join with a Sl st in first sc. Fasten off.

FINISHING

Line Front and Back before sewing. If interfacing is desired for Gusset, pin in place, then line Gusset. Pin Gusset along sides and bottom of Back and Front. Sew in place.

HANDLE (MAKE 2)

With A, ch 7.

ROW 1: Sc in 2nd ch from hook, sc in each ch across, turn. (6 sc)

ROW 2: Ch 1, sc in each sc across, turn.

ROWS 3–158: Rep Row 2. Fasten off, leaving a long sewing length.

Place a marker 18 rows in from each end of each Handle to mark tab that will be sewn to bag. Cut cord into 2 equal parts. Start sewing cord into long strip from marker to marker. Trim cord to fit your Handle. Sew the tab onto bag as pictured.

STARFISH (MAKE 1)

With B, ch 4, join with a Sl st to form a ring.

RND 1: Ch 1, work 10 sc in ring, join with a Sl st in first sc.

RND 2: *Ch 10, Sl st in 2nd ch from hook, sc in next ch, hdc in next ch, dc in each of next 4 ch, tr in each of next 2 ch, sk next sc on Rnd 1, Sl st in next st, rep from * around (5 star points), join with a Sl st in first ch. Fasten off, leaving a long sewing length.

LARGE SAND DOLLAR (MAKE 1)

With A, ch 4, join with Sl st to form a ring.

RND 1: Ch 1, work 10 sc in ring, join with a Sl st in first sc.

RND 2: Ch 1, 2 sc in each sc around, join with a Sl st in first sc. (20 sc)

RND 3: Ch 1, *sc in first sc, 2 sc in next sc, rep from * around, join with a Sl st in first sc. (30 sc)

RND 4: Ch 1, *sc in each of the next 2 sc, 2 sc in next sc, rep from * around, join with a Sl st in first sc. (40 sc) Fasten off, leaving a long sewing length. With E, embroider a Lazy Daisy st of 5 ch sts on top of Sand Dollar.

SMALL SAND DOLLAR (MAKE 3)

With C, work same as Large Sand Dollar through Rnd 3. Fasten off, leaving a sewing length. With E, embroider a Lazy Daisy st of 5 ch sts on top of Sand Dollar.

bottle gift bag

A crocheted bottle carrier makes a really novel way to present a great bottle of Champagne or wine to your favorite hostess. The flower buds add three-dimensional texture, and the drawstring tie cinches the top closed.

Yarn: 4

Tahki Cotton Classic, 100% mercerized cotton, 108 yd (100 m), 1.75 oz (50 g): 1 skein each of #3001 White (A) and #3942 Dark Lavender (B), 2 skeins of #3928 Light Lavender (C)

Hook: F-5 (3.75 mm)

Gauge: Each square = 5" x 5" (12.5 x 12.5 cm)

Finished Size: 5" x 13½" (12.5 x 34.4 cm)

Skill Level: Experienced

SQUARES

Make 4 Flower Bud Squares (page 7) using C for Rnds 1, 2, 3, 5, and 10; A for Rnds 4 and 9; and B for Rnds 6, 7, and 8. Fasten off, leaving a sewing length.

ASSEMBLY

Using whipstitch method (page 115), using B, working on WS, sew squares together into a square, 2 wide by 2 high. Then sew sides together to form a tube.

BOTTOM GUSSET

With RS facing, join C with a Sl st in bottom right-hand corner, work in rounds as follows:

RND 1: Ch 1, work 20 sc evenly spaced across each square to next corner around, join with a Sl st in first sc. (40 sc)

RND 2: Ch 1 *sc in each of next 3 sc, sc2tog, rep from * around, join with a Sl st in first sc. (30 sc)

RND 3: Ch 1, *sc in each of next 2 sc, sc2tog, rep from * around, join with a Sl st in first sc. (20 sc)

RND 4: Ch 1, *sc, sc2tog over next 2 sts, rep from * around, join with a Sl st in first sc. Fasten off, leaving a long sewing length. (10 sc)

Thread tail onto a yarn needle, bring yarn through sts of last rnd, gather, and secure. Fasten off.

TOP BORDER

RND 1: With RS facing, join C with Sl st in top right-hand side, ch 3 (counts as dc here and throughout), dc in each dc across first square, sk seam, dc in each st across second square, join with a Sl st to top of beg ch 3.

RND 2: Ch 4 (counts as dc, ch 1), sk next dc, *dc next dc, ch 1, sk next st, rep from * around, join with a Sl st in 3rd ch of beg ch-4.

RND 3: Ch 1, 2 sc in each ch-1 sp around, join with a Sl st in first sc.

RND 4: Ch 3, dc in each sc around, join with a Sl st in top of beg ch-3.

RND 5: Ch 1, working from left to right, rev sc in each dc around, join with a Sl st in first rev sc. Fasten off C.

DRAWSTRING (MAKE 2)

Using 2 strands of C held together as one, ch 80. Fasten off.

Starting and ending at one side, weave one Drawstring in and out through second row of double crochets around top border. Starting and ending in opposite end, using same spaces as first Drawstring, weave 2nd Drawstring around. Tie ends of each Drawstring together, trim ends.

flower bud amulet

Need a fast little project? An amulet bag is the way to go. This cute little granny bag is a unique way to present a gift card or some other small item, such as jewelry, making it two gifts in one. Or tuck a spare key and a bit of money in it for a quick trip to the coffee shop.

Yarn: (3)
Tahki Cotton Classic Lite, 100% mercerized cotton, 146 yd (135 m), 1.75 oz (50 g): 1 skein each of #4001 White (A), #4803 Sky Blue (B), and #4725 Deep Leaf Green (C)

Hooks: F-5 (3.75 mm) and H-8 (5 mm) for Shoulder Strap only

Notions: 1 large snap, small amount of lining fabric (optional)

Gauge: Each square = 4¼" x 4¼" (11 x 11 cm)

Finished Size: 4½" x 4½" (11.5 x 11.5 cm)

Skill Level: Experienced

SQUARES

With smaller hook, make 2 Flower Bud Squares (page 7) using C for Rnds 1, 2, 3, 5, and 10; A for Rnds 4 and 9; and B for Rnds 6, 7, and 8. Fasten off, leaving a sewing length.

FINISHING

Line both squares using desired lining method. With RS facing, working in back loops only, sew 3 sides of squares together.

STRAP

Cut three 5 yd (4.5 m) lengths of C, using 3 strands held together as one, and larger hook, leaving a sewing length, ch 120. Fasten off, leaving a sewing length. Sew Straps to inside of bag, 1" (2.5 cm) below top along each seam. Sew snap to inside of bag at center top.

LIBELLE DAHLIA

Skill Level: Intermediate

Made with 4 colors: A, B, C, and D.

Picot: Ch 4, sc in 4th ch from hook.

Joining leaf: To join leaf, place hook through picot at point of leaf and through designated st or sp, pick up a loop, and complete a sc.

With A, ch 4, join with a Sl st to form a ring.

RND 1: Ch 4 (counts as a dc, ch 1), [dc, ch 1] 7 times in ring, join with a Sl st in 3rd ch of beg ch 4. Fasten off A. (8 ch-1 sps)

RND 2: With RS facing, join B with Sl st in any ch-1 sp, ch 2 (counts as hdc), (dc, tr, dc, hdc) in same sp, (hdc, dc, tr, dc, hdc) in each ch-1 sp around, join with a Sl st in top of beg ch-2.

RND 3: Ch 1, *2 sc in each of next 4 sts, Sl st in next st, rep from * around, join with a Sl st in first sc. Fasten off B. (8 petals)

RND 4: Working behind petals, with RS facing, join C with a Sl st in any dc between petals in Rnd 1, ch 1, sc in same st, *ch 5, sk next petal, sc in next dc in Rnd 1, rep from * around, ch 5, join with a Sl st in first sc. (8 ch-5 sps)

RND 5: Ch 1, (sc, dc, tr, picot, tr, dc, sc, ch 1) in each ch-5 loop around, join with a Sl st in first sc. (8 leaves)

RND 6: *Ch 5, sk next leaf, sc in next ch-1 sp between leaves, rep from * around, join with a Sl st to first ch of beg ch-5. Fasten off C. (8 ch-5 sps)

RND 7: With RS facing, join D with a Sl st in any ch-5 sp, ch 3 (counts as dc), (2 dc, ch 2, 3 dc) in same ch-5 loop (corner), *ch 2, (dc, sc, joining leaf, dc) in next ch-5 loop, ch 2**, (3 dc, ch 3, 3 dc) in next ch-5 loop (corner), rep from * around, ending last rep at **, join with a Sl st in top of beg ch-3. Fasten off D.

RND 8: With RS facing, join A with a Sl st in any corner ch-2 sp, ch 1, *(2 sc, ch 2, 2 sc) in corner ch-2 sp, [sc in each of next 3 dc, sc in next ch-2 sp] twice, sc in each of next 3 sts, rep from * around, join with a Sl st in first sc. Fasten off A. (15 sc on each side)

RND 9: With RS facing, join B with a Sl st in any corner ch-2 sp, ch 1, *(2 sc, ch 2, 2 sc) in corner ch-2 sp, sc in each of next 15 sc, rep from * around, join with a Sl st in first sc. Fasten off. (19 sc on each side)

BAG 4

knotted tie evening bag

This dressy evening bag is sleek and slim, but still big enough to hold all your necessities. It features Lucite handles, a convenient snap closure, and a fashionable knotted tie. Make one in a color scheme to match your outfit and you'll be the belle of the ball.

Yarn:
Blue Heron Yarns Rayon Loop, 100% rayon, 325 yd (297 m), 8 oz (227 g): 1 hank of Milk Chocolate (A). Blue Heron Yarns Soft Twist Rayon, 100% rayon, 525 yd (480 m), 8 oz (227 g): 1 hank of Milk Chocolate (B)

Hook: F-5 (3.75 mm)

Notions: ½ yd (0.5 m) of lining fabric, 2 Lucite handles or any handles that have a 10" (25.5 cm) opening to attach bag to handle

Gauge: Each square = 4" x 4" (10 x 10 cm); 20 sts = 4" (10 cm)

Finished Size: 11" x 14" (28 x 35.5 cm), including gussets

Skill Level: Experienced

SQUARES

Make 12 Libelle Dahlia Squares (page 16) using B for Rnds 1–7 and A for Rnd 8. Fasten off, leaving a sewing length.

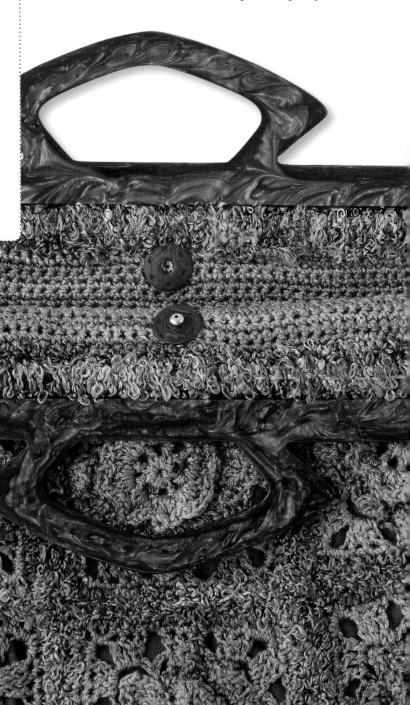

FRONT

Sew 6 squares into a rectangle, 3 wide by 2 high.

ROW 1: With RS facing, join B with Sl st in top right-hand corner, ch 1, work 20 sc evenly spaced across each square, turn. (60 sc)

ROW 2: Ch 1, sc in each sc across, turn.

ROWS 3–8: Rep Row 2, complete last st with A. Fasten off B.

ROWS 9–10: With A, ch 1, sc in each sc across, turn. Fasten off A.

BACK

Sew 6 squares together same as Front.

TIES AND TOP OF BACK

ROW 1: With B, ch 74, join with a Sl st to top right corner of back, ch 1, work 20 sc evenly spaced across each square, ch 75, turn.

ROW 2: Sc in 2nd ch from hook, sc in each ch across, sc in each sc across Back, sc in each ch across second ch, turn. (208 sc)

ROWS 3–8: Ch 1, sc in each sc across, turn. Fasten off B.

ROW 9: With RS facing, join A with Sl st on opposite side of foundation ch on right Tie, ch 1, working across foundation ch, sc in each ch across, working in row-end sts, sc evenly across end of Tie, sc in each st across Row 8, working in row-end sts, sc evenly across end of Tie, working across foundation ch, sc in each ch across, turn.

ROW 10: Ch 1, sc in each sc across. Fasten off A.

GUSSET

With B, ch 8.

ROW 1: Sc in 2nd ch from hook, sc in each ch across, turn. (7 sc)

ROW 2: Ch 1, sc in each sc across, turn.

Rep Row 2 until Gusset fits around 2 sides and bottom of bag. Fasten off B.

FINISHING

Line Back, Front, and Gusset before assembling bag. With RS facing, pin Gusset to Front. With RS facing, join A with Sl st at bottom end of Gusset, working through double thickness, sc evenly across Gusset/Front. With RS facing, pin Gusset to Back. With RS facing, join A with Sl st at bottom end of Gusset, working through double thickness, sc evenly across Gusset/Back.

With yarn needle and A, sew one handle to top of Front and one handle to top of Back. Sew a covered snap (page 123) to the inside of the bag, centered below the handles.

autumn stripes tote

The Libelle Dahlia motif worked in one color makes a lovely, textured square.
Assemble this bag in bold stripes of vibrant autumn hues to create a stunning look.
The snap closure, colorful lining, and smart handles make a stophisticated statement.

Yarn: 3

Tahki Cotton Classic Lite, 100% mercerized cotton, 146 yd (135 m), 1.75 oz (50 g): 3 skeins each of #4405 Tangerine (A) and #4248 Milk Chocolate (B); 2 skeins of #4310 Latte (C), 1 skein of #4002 Black (D)

Hook: F-5 (3.75 mm)

Notions: ¾ yd (0.7 m) of lining fabric, 6" x 36" (15 x 91.5 cm) strip of interfacing, one ¾" (2 cm) snap, 1 pair 24" (61 cm) handles

Gauge: Each square = 4" x 4" (10 x 10 cm); 22 sts and 24 rows sc = 4" (10 cm).

Finished Size: 18" (45.5 cm) wide x 12" (30.5 cm) high, including gussets

Skill Level: Experienced

SQUARES

Make 18 Libelle Dahlia Squares (page 16), making 6 using A, 6 using B, and 6 using C. Fasten off, leaving a sewing length. Using whipstitch method, sew squares together in 6 three-square strips; 2 of each color.

FRONT/BACK (MAKE 2)

Strip Edging:

ROW 1: With RS facing, join D with a Sl st at top left-hand corner of one A Strip, ch 1, *sc in ch-2 sp, sc in each of next 18 sc, sc in corner ch-2 sp**, sk seam, rep from * across, ending last rep at **, turn.

ROW 2: Ch 1, sc in each sc across, turn. Fasten off D.

Starting at the bottom right-hand corner of one C Strip, rep Rows 1–2.

With D, sew A and B Strips together across Strip Edging.

Starting at the top left-hand corner of of B Strip and at the bottom right-hand corner of the C column, rep Strip Edging. With D, sew A and B Strips together across Strip Edging.

(continued)

FIRST GUSSET HALF

Note: Gusset is made in 2 equal parts, one part in A, one part in C, and they are joined together at center bottom.

With A, ch 9.

ROW 1: Sc in 2nd ch from hook, sc in each ch across, turn. (8 sc)

ROW 2: Ch 1, sc in each sc, turn.

ROWS 3–39: Rep Row 2.

ROW 40: Ch 1, sc in first sc, 2 sc in next sc, sc in each sc across to last 2 sc, 2 sc in next sc, sc in last sc, turn. (10 sc)

ROWS 41–45: Rep Row 2.

ROW 46: Rep Row 40. (12 sc)

Continue in this manner, increasing 1 st each end of every 6th row, until there are 28 sts. (At this point, check your work and be sure that the Gusset reaches from center bottom, along bottom and sides up to top. If necessary, add a few more rows of sc.)

SECOND GUSSET HALF

With C, work same as First Gusset Half. With C, sew Gusset Halves together across narrow end.

FINISHING

Before assembling bag, line Back and Front with lining fabric, and prepare Gusset with interfacing and lining. Pin Gusset in place, placing seam at center bottom. Using whipstitch method, sew in place from RS. Cover snap with lining fabric and sew in place inside top center. With sewing needle and matching thread, sew on handles.

amulet with streamers

Amulet bags are popular for gift giving, for little girls' bags, and for evening bags.
These bags take very little yarn and can be made with leftovers in many different colors.
The streamers add a bit of whimsy and can be made as long or as short as you want.

Yarn:
Tahki Cotton Classic, 100% mercerized cotton, 108 yd (100 m), 1.75 oz (50 g): 1 skein each of #3701 Light Cactus Green (A), #3783 Bright Teal (B), and #3913 Deep Red-Violet (C)

Hooks: F-5 (3.75 mm) and H-8 (5 mm) for Shoulder Strap only

Notions: 1 large snap, small amount of lining fabric (optional)

Gauge: Each square = 3¾" x 3¾" (9.5 x 9.5 cm)

Finished Size: 4" x 4" (10 x 10 cm)

Skill Level: Experienced

SQUARES

With smaller hook, make 2 Libelle Dahlia Squares (page 16) using B for Rnds 1, 6, and 7; C for Rnds 2 and 8; and A for Rnds 3–5. Fasten off, leaving a sewing length.

FINISHING

Line both squares using desired lining method. With RS facing, working in back loops only, sew 3 sides of squares together.

STRAP

With 2 strands of C held together as one and larger hook, leaving a sewing length, ch 120. Fasten off, leaving a sewing length. Sew one end of Strap to inside of bag, 1" (2.5 cm) below top along each seam. Sew snap to inside of bag at center top.

BUD VINE FRINGE

Note: Make 2 using C, 1 using B, and 1 using A.

Leaving a sewing length, *ch 16, (5 dc, ch 2, Sl st) in 4th ch from hook, rep from * 3 times. Fasten off.

Sew beginning end of Fringes to bottom corners of bag as pictured.

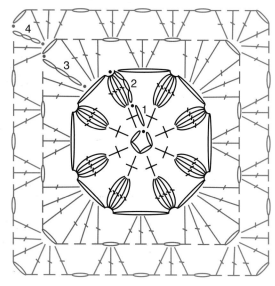

BLOOMING GRANNY

Skill Level: Easy

Made with 3 colors: A, B, and C.

Popcorn (pc): Make 5 dc in specified st, draw up the last loop slightly and remove hook, insert hook in the first of the 5 dc made, pick up the dropped loop and draw it through, ch 1.

With A, ch 4, join with a Sl st to form a ring.

RND 1: With A, ch 1, 8 sc in ring, join with a Sl st in first sc.

RND 2: (pc rnd): With A, ch 3 (counts as a dc), 4 dc in first st, insert hook in the top of the ch 3, pick up dropped loop, tighten, ch 1 to complete first pc, ch 1, *pc in next sc, ch 1, rep from * 6 times more (8 pc), join with a Sl st to top of the beg ch-3, fasten off A.

RND 3: Join B in any ch-1 sp, ch 3 (counts as a dc now and throughout), 2 dc in same sp (half corner), *ch 1, 3 dc next ch-1 sp, ch 1**, [3 dc, ch 1, 3 dc] next ch-1 sp (corner), rep from * twice, rep from * to **, 3 dc in same sp as beg half corner, ch 1, join with a Sl st to top of beg ch-3 (this completes first corner), fasten off B.

RND 4: Join C in any corner ch-1 sp, ch 3, 2 dc in same sp (half corner), *[ch 1, 3 dc next ch-1 sp] twice, ch 1**, [3 dc, ch 1, 3 dc] in next ch-1 sp (corner), ch 1, rep from * twice, rep from * to ** once, 3 dc in same sp as beg half corner, ch 1, join with a Sl st to top of beg ch 3 (this completes first corner), fasten off.

tablet cover

Protect your tablet or iPad with this colorful cover. It closes with two simple button loops, and the back has a handy pocket to stow your stylus.

Yarn:  4

Universal Yarns Cotton Supreme, 100% cotton, 180 yd (165 m), 3.5 oz (100 g): 1 hank each of #513 Purple (A), #618 Lime (B), #516 Aqua (C), and #606 Lavender (D)

Hook: G-6 (4 mm)

Notions: Two ¾" (2 cm) buttons

Gauge: Each square = 3½" x 3½" (9.5 x 9.5 cm); 15 sts and 9 rows dc = 4" (10 cm)

Finished Size: 10½" (26.5 cm) wide x 7" (18 cm) high

Skill Level: Easy

FRONT

Make 6 Blooming Granny Squares (page 26) in the following color sequences:

Square A (make 3): Use C for Rnds 1 and 2, B for Rnd 3, and A for Rnd 4. Fasten off, leaving a sewing length.

Square B (make 3): Use D for Rnds 1 and 2, B for Rnd 3, and A for Rnd 4. Fasten off, leaving a sewing length.

Using whipstitch method, sew squares together in a rectangle, 3 wide by 2 high as pictured.

BACK

With A, ch 39.

ROW 1: Dc in 3rd ch from hook, dc in each ch across, turn. (38 dc)

ROW 2: Ch 3 (counts as dc here and throughout), dc in each dc across, turn. Fasten off A, join C.

ROWS 3–16: Rep Row 2, working 2 rows each of C, B, D, A, C, B, D. Fasten off D.

BACK POCKET

With C, ch 11.

ROW 1: Dc in 3rd ch from hook, dc in each ch across, turn. (10 dc)

ROW 2: Ch 3 (counts as dc here and throughout), dc in each dc across, turn. Fasten off C, join B.

ROWS 3–10: Rep Row 2, working 2 rows each of B, D, A, C. Fasten off C.

Pocket Edging

ROW 1: With RS facing, join A with Sl st in bottom right-hand corner, ch 1, sc evenly up side edge, across top, and down other side edge; do not turn.

ROW 2: Ch 1, working from left to right, rev sc in each sc across 3 sides of pocket. Fasten off, leaving a long sewing length. Aligning stripes with Back, pin Pocket in place on Back, 1 ½" (3.8 cm) in from left side. With sewing length, sew in place.

Using whipstitch method, sew Back to Front.

TOP EDGING

RND 1: With RS facing, join A with Sl st in top right-hand corner, ch 1, sc evenly around top opening, join with a Sl st in first sc.

RND 2: Ch 1, rev sc in each sc around top, join with a Sl st in first rev sc. Fasten off A.

BUTTON LOOPS (MAKE 2)

Mark Back to correspond with seams between top squares. Cut a 2 yd (1.8 m) length of A, fold length in half, draw this length through marked st and secure. Using 2 strands held together as one, ch 20, Sl st in same place as joining. Fasten off A. Sew buttons 1" (2.5 cm) below top edge on Front at seams.

BAG 8

drawstring pouch

Granny squares accent the bottom of this lovely drawstring bag. Contrast lining peeks through the crochet mesh of the bag body. Little flowers (from the square center) add a pretty touch and prevent the drawstring ends from pulling through the cord stop.

Yarn: 4

LB Collection Crepe Twist, 88% wool, 12% nylon, 112 yd (102 m), 1.75 oz (50 g): 3 hanks of #191 Plum (A)

LB Collection Superwash Merino, 100% merino wool, 306 yd (280 m), 3.50 oz (100 g): 1 skein #102 Aqua (B)

Hooks: F-5 (3.75 mm) and H-8 (5 mm) for Shoulder Strap and Drawstring

Notions: 1 cord stop, ½ yd (0.5 m) of lining fabric

Gauge: With smaller hook, each square = 3" x 3" (7.5 x 7.5 cm); 16 sts and 14 rows hdc = 4" (10 cm)

Finished Size: 11" (28 cm) wide x 12" (20.5 cm) high

Skill Level: Easy

SQUARES

With smaller hook, make 8 Blooming Granny Squares (page 26) using A for Rnds 1, 2, and 4 and B for Rnd 3. Fasten off, leaving a sewing length.

Sew squares together in 2 strips, 4 wide for Back and 4 wide for Front. Sew Front to Back across sides and bottom.

BODY OF BAG

RND 1: With RS facing, join A with a Sl st in corner ch-1 sp of first square on Front, ch 3 (counts as hdc, ch 1 here and throughout), sk next st, hdc in next dc, *[ch 1, sk next st, hdc in next dc] 5 times, sk seam, rep from * around, ch 1, join with a Sl st to 2nd ch of beg ch-3. (56 ch-1 sps)

RND 2: Ch 3, (hdc, ch 1) in each hdc around, join with a Sl st in 2nd ch of beg ch-3.

RNDS 3–28: Rep Rnd 2. Fasten off A.

RND 29: With RS facing, join B with a Sl st in first ch-1 sp, ch 1, 2 sc in each ch-1 sp around, join with a Sl st in first sc. Fasten off B.

(continued)

SHOULDER STRAP

Place a marker on each side at top of bag for Strap placement. Cut 4 strands of yarn B, 12 yd (11 m) each. Using all 4 strands held together as one and larger hook, ch 200. Fasten off. Pull one end of Shoulder Strap through a ch-1 sp on one side of bag, bring end around, and pull through ch-1 sp on other side. Tie a secure knot. Hide knot in the space at top of bag.

FLOWER (MAKE 2)

With B and smaller hook, leaving a sewing length to begin, work Blooming Granny Square through Rnd 2. Fasten off. Set aside.

DRAWSTRING

With 2 strands of B held together as one and larger hook, ch 120. Starting in ch-1 sp at center front of bag, in the 2nd row below top edge of bag, weave Drawstring in and out of ch-1 sps around bag. Pull ends of Drawstring through the cord stop. Sew one Flower to each end of Drawstring.

LINING

Cut lining fabric to 13" x 24" (33 x 61 cm). With WS together, fold fabric in half crosswise. Sew 2 sides, forming a pouch. Place lining into bag with seams at sides. Turn top edges under, pin in place, and sew lining to top of bag.

granny pocket tote

On this bag, a block of Blooming Granny Squares makes a front pocket, turning an ordinary crocheted tote into something special. The toggle button adds a simple but elegant design element, and an analogous color scheme of warm, neutral tones lends an air of contemporary sophistication.

Yarn: 🧶 2

Lucci Yarns 2000 Hemp, 100% hemp, 220 yd (201 m), 2.75 oz (50 g): 3 balls of Foggy (A), 1 ball each of Pearl (B) and Charcoal (C)

Hook: E-4 (3.5 mm)

Notions: One 1¾" (4.5 cm) toggle button, ½ yd (0.5 m) of lining fabric, 1½" x 34" (3.8 x 86.5 cm) strip single-sided fusible interfacing for Gusset (optional), ½ yd (0.5 m) of drapery cord to line Handle

Finished Size: 18½" (47 cm) wide x 10" (25.5 cm) high

Gauge: Each square = 3" x 3" (7.5 x 7.5 cm); 16 sts and 8 rows hdc = 4" (10 cm)

Skill Level: Easy

POCKET

Make 6 Blooming Granny Squares (page 26) using B for Rnds 1 and 2, A for Rnd 3, and C for Rnd 4. Fasten off, leaving a sewing length.

Using whipstitch method, sew squares into a rectangle, 3 wide by 2 high.

Pocket Edging

Note: Skip joined corner sps and seams when working Edging Rnd 1.

RND 1: With RS facing, join A with a Sl st in bottom right-hand corner, ch 1, *(2 sc, ch 1, 2 sc) in corner sp, sk next dc, dc in each dc across to 1 dc before next corner, rep from * around, join with a Sl st in top of first sc. Set aside.

FRONT/BACK (MAKE 2)

With A, ch 65.

Note: When making increases, make increase in 2nd st in from each end of row.

ROW 1: Hdc in 3rd ch from hook, hdc in each ch across, turn. (64 hdc)

ROW 2: Ch 2 (counts as hdc here and throughout), hdc in each st across, turn.

Rep Row 2, increasing 1 st at each end of row, every 1½" (3.8 cm), 5 times. (74 hdc at end of last row)

Work even on 74 hdc until piece measures 10" (25.5 cm) from beg. Fasten off A.

(continued)

GUSSET

With A, ch 10.

ROW 1: Hdc in 3rd ch from hook, hdc in each ch across, turn. (9 hdc)

ROW 2: Ch 2 (counts as hdc here and throughout), hdc in each hdc across, turn.

Rep Row 2 until Gusset measures 34" (86.5 cm) from beg. Fasten off, leaving a long sewing length.

FINISHING

Line Back, Front, and Pocket. If interfacing is used, place interfacing on Gusset and press into place, then line Gusset. With RS facing up, center Pocket on Front, 2½" (6.5 cm) above bottom edge, sew in place. With WS together, pin Gusset to Front and Back panels. With RS facing, join A with a Sl st in top left-hand corner of Front, working through double thickness of Front and Gusset, sc in each st across side, bottom, and 2nd side. Fasten off A. Join Gusset to Back in same manner.

BUTTON LOOP

Cut a 2 yd (1.8 m) length of A. Fold length in half, and draw through center stitch on top back and secure. Using doubled strand, ch 20. Fasten off, leaving a sewing length. Sew to same st as joining to form a loop. Sew button to Front opposite Button Loop.

HANDLE (MAKE 2)

With A, ch 8.

ROW 1: Sc in 2nd ch from hook, sc in each ch across, turn. (7 sc)

ROW 2: Ch 1, sc in each sc across, turn.

Rep Row 2 until Handle measures 20" (51 cm) from beg. Fasten off, leaving a sewing length.

Cut drapery cord in half, laying length on one Handle, sew Handle around cord, forming a tube (see page 120), leaving 1½" (3.8 cm) at each end unjoined for tabs. Repeat for other Handle. Placing tabs at sides of pocket, sew one Handle in place on Front. Sew other Handle to Back in same position.

SUNFLOWER

Skill Level: Experienced

Made with 4 colors: A, B, C, and D.

Bubble Stitch (BS): Alternate single and triple crochet stitches worked from the wrong side in designated stitch or sp.

Picot: Ch 3, Sl st in 3rd ch from hook.

With A, form an adjustable loop ring.

RND 1: Ch 3 (counts as dc), 11 dc into ring, join with a Sl st in top of beg ch-3, turn. Tighten ring. (12 dc)

RND 2: With WS facing, ch 1, starting in first st, (sc, tr) (BS) in each st around, join with a Sl st in first sc. Place a marker in first st of rnd and move marker up as work progresses. (12 BS/24 sts)

RND 3: With WS facing, ch 1, (sc, tr, sc) in first st (BS), *sk next tr, (sc, tr, sc) in next sc, rep from * around, sk last tr, join with a Sl st in first sc. (12 BS/36 sts)

RND 4: Ch 1, sc in first st, *sk next tr, (sc, tr) in next sc**, sc in next sc, rep from * around, ending last rep at **, join with a Sl st in first sc, turn. Fasten off A. (12 BS/36 sts)

RND 5: With RS facing, join B with a Sl st in first st, ch 1, sc in first st, *ch 2, sk next st, sc next st, rep from * around, ch 2, join with a Sl st in first sc. (18 ch-2 sps)

RND 6: Ch 1, *sc in next ch-2 sp, (sc, hdc, 2 dc, tr, picot) in the next ch-2 sp (tr, 2 dc, hdc, sc) in next ch-2 sp, rep from * around, join with a Sl st in first sc. Fasten off B. (6 petals)

RND 7: Working behind petals, with RS facing, join C with a Sl st in any sc between 2 petals, *ch 4, sk next sc, sc in next sc in Rnd 5 at center of next petal, ch 4**, sc in next sc between petals, rep from * around, ending last rep at **, join with a Sl st in first sc. (12 ch-4 loops)

RND 8: Ch 1, *4 sc in next ch-4 loop, (sc, hdc, 2 dc, 2 tr, picot) in next ch-4 loop, (2 tr, 2 dc, hdc, sc) in next ch-4 loop**, 4 sc in next ch-4 loop, rep from * around, ending last rep at **, join with a Sl st in first sc. Fasten off C.

RND 9: With RS facing, join D with a Sl st in any corner picot, ch 1, *(2 sc, ch 2, 2 sc) in corner picot, sc in each of the next 5

sts, hdc in each of the next 6 sc, sc in each of next 5 sts**, rep from * around, join with a Sl st in first sc. (20 sts on each side)

RND 10: Sl st to corner ch-2 sp, ch 2 (counts as dc), (dc, ch 2, 2 dc) in corner ch-2 sp, *ch 2, sk next 3 sts, dc in each of next 2 sts, [ch 2, sk next 2 sts, dc in each of next 2 sts] 3 times, ch 2, sk next 3 sts**, (2 dc, ch 2, 2 dc) in next ch-2 sp, rep from * around, ending last rep at **, join with a Sl st in top of beg ch-3. Fasten off D.

RND 11: With RS facing, join B with a Sl st in any corner ch-2 sp, ch 1, *(2 sc, ch 2, 2 sc) in corner ch-2 sp, [sc in each of the next 2 dc, 2 sc in next ch-2 sp] 5 times, sc in each of the 2 dc, rep from * around, join with a Sl st in first sc. Fasten off B.

RND 12: With RS facing, join A with a Sl st in any corner ch-2 sp, ch 1, *(2 sc, ch 2, 2 sc) in corner ch-2 sp, sc in each of next 28 sts, rep from * around, join with a Sl st in first sc. Fasten off A.

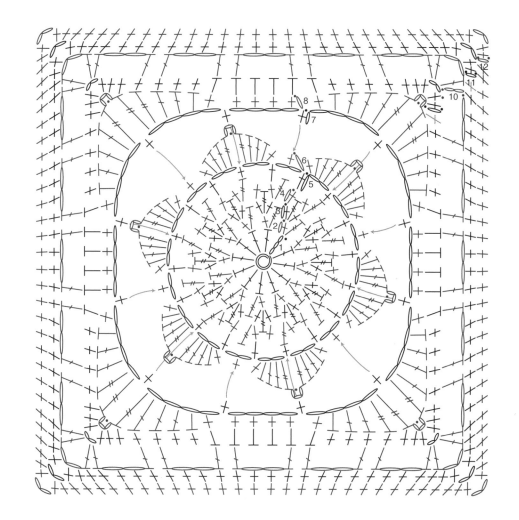

project tote

The beautiful yarn and unusual color combination make this tote really eye-catching, perfect for carrying your crochet projects. The variegated yarn lends interest and texture and the wooden handles give it a classic, sophisticated flair.

Yarn: ⓷

Blue Heron Yarn Cotton Ray Seed, 68% rayon, 32% cotton, 475 yd (434 m), 8 oz (227 g): 1 hank each of Bluegrass (A) and Iris (B)

Hook: F-5 (3.75 mm)

Notions: 1 wooden bag handle with 8" (20.5 cm) opening, ¾ yd (0.7 m) of lining fabric

Gauge: Each square = 6" x 6" (15 x 15 cm); 20 sts and 8 rows in dc = 4" (10 cm)

Finished Size: 18" (45.5 cm) wide x 14" (35.5 cm) high, excluding handles

Skill Level: Experienced

SQUARES

Make 12 Sunflower Squares (page 38) using A for Rnds 1–6 and B for Rnds 7–12. Fasten off, leaving a sewing length.

FRONT/BACK (MAKE 2)

Using whipstich method on WS, using B, sew 6 squares into a rectangle, 3 wide by 2 high. Line the 6 squares while flat, before adding the top panel.

TOP PANEL

With RS facing, join A with a Sl st in top right corner.

ROW 1: Ch 3 (counts as dc here and throughout), work 29 dc evenly spaced across first square, work 30 dc evenly spaced across next 3 squares, turn. (90 dc)

ROW 2: Ch 3, dc in each next 7 dc, dc2tog over next 2 sts, *dc in each next 8, dc2tog over next 2 sts, rep from * across, turn. (81 dc)

ROW 3: Ch 3, dc in each next 6 dc, dc2tog over next 2 sts, *dc in each next 7, dc2tog over next 2 sts, rep from * across, turn. (72 dc)

ROW 4: Ch 3, dc in each next 5 dc, dc2tog over next 2 sts, *dc in each next 6, dc2tog over next 2 sts, rep from * across, turn. (63 dc)

ROW 5: Ch 3, dc in each next 4 dc, dc2tog over next 2 sts, *dc in each next 5, dc2tog over next 2 sts, rep from * across, turn. (54 dc)

ROW 6: Ch 3, dc in each next 3 dc, dc2tog over next 2 sts, *dc in each next 4, dc2tog over next 2 sts, rep from * across, turn. (45 dc)

ROW 7: Ch 3, dc in each next 2 dc, dc2tog over next 2 sts, *dc in each next 3, dc2tog over next 2 sts, rep from * across, turn. (36 dc)

ROWS 8–9: Ch 3, dc in each dc across. Fasten off, leaving a long sewing length.

FINISHING

Sew Front to Back across sides and bottom of squares only, leaving Top Panel loose.

Pull last 2 rows of Top Panel through bag handle slit, sew down on WS.

bead handle clutch

The Blue Heron Yarn used for the Project Tote (page 40) has such great yardage per skein that there is enough left over to make this little evening clutch. Featuring a beaded strap, diamond-oriented squares, and discrete snap closure, the clutch is reminiscent of an elegant envelope.

Yarn: ③

Blue Heron Yarn, Cotton Rayon Seed, 68% rayon, 32% cotton, 475 yd (434 m), 8 oz (227 g): 1 skein each of Bluegrass (A) and Iris (B)

Hook: F-5 (3.75 mm)

Notions: ¼ yd (0.25 m) of felt for inner lining, ¼ yd (0.25 m) of lining fabric, 1 large snap covered with lining fabric, silk beading thread, two 12" (30.5 cm) strands of glass pearls, one 7" (18 cm) strand of 8mm crystals, one 7" (18 cm) strand of 10mm glass beads (optional, to be used to create beaded Strap)

Gauge: Each square = 6½" x 6½" (16.5 x 16.5 cm)

Finished Size: 8" (20.5 cm) wide x 9" (23 cm) high

Skill Level: Experienced

SQUARES

Make 4 Sunflower Squares (page 38) using A for Rnds 1–6 and B for Rnds 7–12. Fasten off B. Then work one more rnd as follows:

RND 13: With RS facing, join A with a Sl st in any corner ch-2 sp, ch 3, dc in same sp, *sk next st, dc in each of the next 28 sc**, (2 dc, ch 2, 2 dc) in next corner ch-2 sp, rep from * around, ending last rep at **, 2 dc in same sp as joining, ch 2, join with a Sl st in top of beg ch-3. Fasten off, leaving a sewing length.

Using whipstich method, working on WS, sew squares together into a square, 2 wide by 2 high.

FINISHING

Line the 4 squares while flat, first with the felt to add body, then line with lining fabric. Fold into an envelope shape, sew side seams following Assembly Diagram. Cover a large snap following directions on page 123. Sew snap in place. Create and attach 2 handles with silk beading thread and beads (see page 121).

ASSEMBLY DIAGRAMS

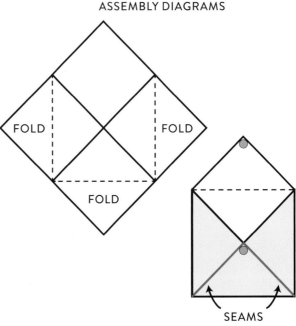

FOLD · FOLD · FOLD

SEAMS

playful pouch

Any little girl would love this colorful pouch to carry her special possessions. The yarns are so bright and cheerful! This pouch features a sweet drawstring closure and lovely round shape.

Yarn:

Lion Brand Modern Baby, 50% acrylic, 50% nylon, 173 yd (158 m), 2.6 oz (75 g): 1 skein each of #133 Orange (A), #158 Bright Yellow (B), #109 Blue (C), and #130 Green (D)

Notions: ½ yd (0.5 m) of lining fabric

Hook: H-8 (5 mm)

Gauge: Each square = 7" x 7" (18 x 18 cm)

Finished Size: 14" (35.5 cm) wide x 12" (30.5 cm) high, including top border

Skill Level: Experienced

SQUARES

Make 5 Sunflower Squares (page 38) using A for Rnds 1, 2, 3, 4, and 12; B for Rnds 5, 6, and 11; C for Rnds 7 and 8; and D for Rnds 9 and 10. Fasten off, leaving a sewing length.

Using whipstich method, working from WS, sew 4 squares together in a strip. Line while flat, then sew ends together, forming a tube. Line the 5th square while flat. Sew 5th square to bottom of 4 assembled squares.

TOP BORDER

RND 1: With RS facing, join A with a SI st in any corner ch-2 sp on top edge, ch 4 (counts as dc, ch 1 here and throughout), sk next st, *dc in next st, ch 1, sk next st, rep from * around, join with a SI st in 3rd ch of beg ch-4.

RND 2: Ch 1, 2 sc in each ch-1 sp around, join with a SI st in first sc.

RND 3: Ch 4, *sk next 2 sts, (dc, ch 2, dc) in next sc, rep from * around to last 3 sts, sk next 3 sts, dc in same sc as join, ch 2, join with a SI st in 3rd ch of beg ch-4.

RND 4: Ch 3, 3 dc in each ch-2 sp around, 2 dc in last ch-2 sp, join with a SI st in top of beg ch-3.

RND 5: Ch 1, working from left to right, rev sc in each dc around, join with a SI st in first rev sc. Fasten off.

DRAWSTRINGS (MAKE 2)

Using 2 strands of A held together as one, ch 90. Fasten off.

Fold bag so that there is one full square facing front and one half-square on each side. Place marker at the center of each side. Starting and ending at one marker, weave one Drawstring in and out of the open spaces in Rnd 1. Tie ends in an overhand knot. Starting and ending at other marker, weave other Drawstring in and out of the same spaces in Rnd 1. Tie ends in an overhand knot. When Drawstrings are pulled they will close the bag.

TRICOLOR CLUSTER

Skill Level: Experienced

Made with 3 colors: A, B, and C.

Double crochet 5 together (dc5tog): (Yo, draw up loop in next st, yo, draw through 2 loops on hook) 5 times, yo and draw through 6 loops on hook.

Double crochet 6 together (dc6tog): (Yo, draw up loop in next st, yo, draw through 2 loops on hook) 6 times, yo and draw through 7 loops on hook.

On rounds 3 and 5 you will be working into sts 2 rows below.

With A, ch 8, join with a Sl st to form a ring.

RND 1: With A, ch 3 (counts as dc here and throughout), 5 dc in ring, [ch 3, 6 dc] 3 times in ring, ch 3, join with a Sl st in 3rd ch of beg ch-3. (4 ch-3 sps)

RND 2: With A, ch 3, dc5tog worked across next 5 sts, *ch 5, Sl st in 2nd ch of next ch-3 sp, ch 5**, dc6tog worked across next 6 sts, rep from * twice, rep from * to ** once, join with a Sl st to 3rd ch of beg ch-3, drop A to WS. Do not fasten off. (4 clusters, 8 ch-5 sps)

RND 3: With RS facing, join B in top of any cluster, *working over sts in Rnd 2, work (3 dc, ch 1, 3 dc, ch 2, 3 dc, ch 1, 3 dc) in next ch-3 sp in Rnd 1, Sl st in top of next cluster, rep from * 3 times more, working last Sl st in the same place as joining, pick up A. Fasten off B. (4 ch-2 sps)

RND 4: With A, ch 3, 5 dc in the first st, *sk next (3 dc, ch 1, 3 dc), work (6 dc, ch 2, 6 dc) in next ch-2 sp, sk next (3 dc, ch 1, 3 dc)**, 6 dc in Sl st in top of next cluster, rep from * twice, rep from * to **, join with a Sl st in 3rd ch of beg ch-3. Fasten off A. (4 ch-2 sps)

RND 5: With RS facing, join C in last Sl st of Rnd 4, ch 1, 1 sc in first dc, 1 sc in each of next 5 dc, *working over sts in Rnd 4, 1 sc in next ch-1 sp between the groups of dc in Rnd 3, 1 sc in each of the next 6 dc, 3 sc in next ch-2 sp, 1 sc in each of next 6 dc, working over sts in Rnd 4, 1 sc in next ch-1 sp between the groups of dc in Rnd 3**, 1 sc in each of next 6 dc, rep from * twice, rep from * to ** once, join with a Sl st in first sc. (92 sc)

RND 6: With C, ch 3 (counts as dc), 1 dc in each of next 13 sc, *3 dc in next sc, 1 dc in each of next 22 sc, rep from * twice, 3 dc in next sc, dc in each of next 8 sc, join with a Sl st in 3rd ch of beg ch-3. Fasten off. (100 dc)

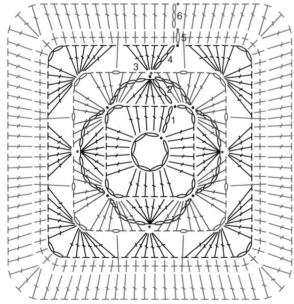

BAG 13

origami folds

Turn 16 granny squares into this uniquely shaped bag. The folds open up to make a surprisingly roomy tote. The bamboo handles are a perfect foil for the lush jewel tones, which evoke the serene naturalism of Monet's famous *Water Lilies*.

Yarn: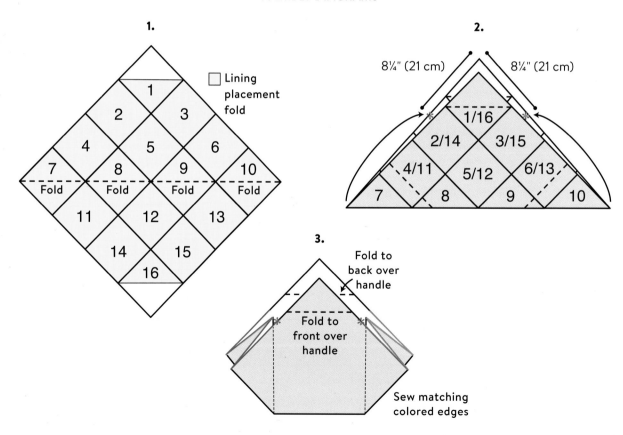

Berroco Weekend, 75% acrylic, 25% Peruvian cotton, 205 yd (189 m), 3.5 oz (100 g): 2 hanks each of #5967 Lilac (A) and #5983 Cottage (B), 1 hank of #5981 Seedling (C)

Hook: F-5 (3.75 mm)

Notions: 1 pair 7" (18 cm) circular bamboo bag handles

Gauge: Each square = 5½" x 5½" (14 x 14 cm)

Finished Size: 21" (53.5 cm) wide x 12" (30.5 cm) high

Skill Level: Experienced

SQUARES

Make 16 Tricolor Cluster Squares (page 46) using A for Rnds 1, 2, and 4; C for Rnd 3; and B for Rnds 5 and 6. Fasten off, leaving a sewing length. Using weave seam method, sew squares together into a square, 4 wide by 4 deep.

ASSEMBLY DIAGRAMS

1.

Lining placement fold

1 2 3 4 5 6 7 8 9 10
Fold Fold Fold Fold
11 12 13 14 15 16

2.

8¼" (21 cm)   8¼" (21 cm)

1/16
2/14 3/15
4/11 5/12 6/13
7 8 9 10

3.

Fold to back over handle

Fold to front over handle

Sew matching colored edges

FINISHING

To line this bag, cut lining about ½" (1.3 cm) larger than square all around. Trim off 2 opposing corners, leaving seam allowance. Turn edges of lining under and sew in place, leaving 2 opposing corners unlined. Fold the 2 unlined points together and pin. These points will be turned down over the handles. Measure 8 ¼" (21 cm) on each side from the free points and place markers. Fold the points of sides into bag and pin the free points to each marker. Sew the sides, forming gussets, following Assembly Diagram. Remove markers. Remove pins from the unlined points, and turn the flaps to the outside over the handles. Bring the top points over handles and sew in place.

BAG 14

gusseted linen bag

The yarn used for this bag is 100 percent wet-spun linen and is surprisingly strong, just right for bag making. The two granny square pockets on the gusset add interest and are great for keeping a cell phone or keys handy.

Yarn: 〔3〕

Louet Euroflax Sport, 100% wet-spun linen, 270 yd (246 m), 3.5 oz (100 g): 2 hanks of #2444 Sandalwood (A), 1 hank each of #2024 Ginger (B) and #2014 Champagne (C)

Hooks: E-4 (3.5 mm) and G-6 (4 mm) for Button Loop only

Notions: 1 pair 6" (15 cm) bamboo bag handles, one 2" (5 cm) toggle button, ½ yd (0.5 m) of lining fabric, 4" x 36" (10 x 91 cm) strip of interfacing

Gauge: Each square = 3 ½" x 3 ½" (9 x 9 cm); 26 sts and 12 rows dc = 4" (10 cm)

Finished Size: 17½" (44.5 cm) wide x 12" (30.5 cm) tall, including gusset

Skill Level: Experienced

SQUARES

Make 26 Tricolor Cluster Squares (page 46) using C for Rnds 1, 2, and 4; B for Rnd 3; and A for Rnds 5 and 6. Fasten off, leaving a sewing length.

(continued)

GUSSET

With A, ch 25.

ROW 1: Dc in 3rd ch from hook, dc in each ch across, turn. (24 dc)

ROW 2: Ch 3 (counts as dc here and throughout), dc in each dc across, turn.

Rep Row 2 until piece measures 35" (89 cm). Fasten off.

FRONT/BACK (MAKE 2)

Using weave seam method, sew squares together into a rectangle, 4 wide by 3 deep. To line bag, cut lining fabric about ½" (1.3 cm) larger than Front/Back. Folding ½" (1.3 cm) to inside, pin in place, then sew lining in place. Line Gusset as shown (page 118). When pieces are lined, pin Gusset in place. Sew Gusset to Front and Back from RS. Place remaining 2 squares on Gusset, aligned with bottom square of Front. Sew in place around sides and bottom edges to form pockets.

TOP BORDER

With RS facing, join A with a Sl st at one side of Gusset, ch 1, *work in sps between sts on Gusset, sc in each sp between sts across top of Gusset, work across top edge of Front/Back, sc in each dc across to next Gusset, sk the ch sp and the seam sts, rep from * once, join with a Sl st in first sc. Fasten off A.

BUTTON LOOP

Cut two 2 yd (1.8 m) lengths of A. Fold strands in half, using larger hook, draw the strands through the center seam st of Back and secure. Using all 4 strands, ch 20, slip st in same place as joining.

Sew on handles, sew on toggle button on Front opposite Button Loop.

uptown tote

This midsize handbag will take you from day to evening with ease. It is the perfect accessory for your little black dress. Go bold with the bright royal blue and plum featured here, or change up the colors to match your accessories. Either way, you and your tote will make a fashionable entrance.

Yarn: 〔4〕

Lion Brand Crepe Twist, 88% wool, 12% nylon, 112 yd (102 m), 1.75 oz (50 g): 1 hank each of #109 Royal (A) and #191 Plum (B), 3 hanks of #153 Black (C)

Hook: G-6 (4 mm)

Notions: ¾ yd (0.7 m) of lining fabric, 1" x 38" (2.5 x 96.5 cm) strip of single-side adhesive interfacing for Gusset, 1 Velcro snap, 1 pair 18" (45.5 cm) handles

Gauge: Each square = 5" x 5" (12.5 x 12.5 cm); 18 sts and 8 rows dc = 4" (10 cm)

Finished Size: 18" (45.5 cm) wide x 8½" (21.5 cm) high, excluding Gusset

Skill Level: Experienced

SQUARES

Make 6 Tricolor Cluster Squares (page 46) using C for Rnds 1, 2, and 6; B for Rnds 3 and 5; and A for Rnd 4. Fasten off, leaving a sewing length.

FRONT/BACK (MAKE 2)

Sew 3 squares together into a strip.

Bottom Striping

ROW 1: With RS facing, join C with a Sl st in bottom right-hand corner dc, ch 3 (counts as dc here and throughout), dc in each dc across each square, sk the seams, turn. (78 dc)

ROW 2: Ch 3, dc in each dc across, turn. Fasten off C, join B.

ROW 3: With B, rep Row 2.

ROW 4: Ch 3, 2 dc in next dc, dc in each st across to last 2 dc, 2 dc in next st, dc in last dc, turn. Fasten off B, join A. (80 dc)

ROW 5: With A, rep Row 2.

ROW 6: Rep Row 4. Fasten off A, join C. (82 dc)

ROWS 7–8: With C, rep Row 2. Fasten off.

(continued)

GUSSET

With C, ch 8.

ROW 1: Dc in 3rd ch from hook, dc in each ch across, turn. (6 dc)

ROW 2: Ch 3, dc in each dc across, turn.

Rep Row 2 until Gusset measures 36" (91.5 cm) from beg.

FINISHING

Before assembling bag, line Back and Front with lining fabric. Line Gusset with interfacing and lining fabric as shown on page 118. When pieces are lined, pin Gusset in place. Sew Gusset to Front and Back from RS. Sew Velcro snap to top center inside of bag. Sew on handles.

PAULA'S PENDANT

Skill Level: Experienced

Made with 5 colors: A, B, C, D, and E.

With A, ch 4, join with a Sl st to form a ring.

RND 1: With A, ch 3 (counts as dc here and throughout), 1 dc in ring, [ch 1, 2 dc] 5 times in ring, ch 1, join with a Sl st in 3rd ch of beg ch-3. Fasten off A. (6 ch-1 sps)

RND 2: With RS facing, join B in any ch-1 sp, ch 3, (1 dc, ch 1, 2 dc) in same sp, (2 dc, ch 1, 2 dc) in each ch-1 sp around, join with a Sl st in 3rd ch of beg ch-3. Fasten off B. (6 shells)

RND 3: With RS facing, join C in any ch-1 sp, ch 3, 6 dc in same sp, 7 dc in each ch-1 sp around, join with a Sl st to 3rd ch of beg ch-3. Fasten off C. (6 shells)

RND 4: With RS facing, join D in first dc of any shell, starting in same st, *1 sc in each of next 7 dc, working over sts in Rnd 3, 1 dc in the sp between 2 shells in Rnd 2, rep from * 5 times, join with a Sl st in first sc. Fasten off D. (42 sc)

RND 5: With RS facing, join E in first st, ch 1, starting in same st, 1 sc in each of next 7 sc, *(1 dc, ch 2, 1 dc) in next dc (corner made)**, 1 sc in each of next 11 sc, rep from * twice, rep from * to ** once, 1 sc in each of next 4 sc, join with a Sl st in first sc. (44 sc, 8 dc, 4 ch-2 sps)

RND 6: With E, ch 1, starting in same st, 1 sc in each on next 5 sc, 1 hdc in each of next 4 sc, *(2 dc, ch 3, 2 dc) in next ch-2 sp (corner made), 1 hdc in each of next 4 sc**, 1 sc in each of next 5 sc, 1 hdc in each of next 4, rep from * twice, rep from * to ** once, 1 sc in next sc, join with a Sl st to first sc. (17 sts across each side, 4 ch-3 corner sps)

RND 7: Ch 3, 1 dc in each next 9 sts, *(2 dc, ch 3, 2 dc) in next ch-3 sp (corner)**, 1 dc in each of next 17 sts, rep from * twice, rep from * to **, 1 dc in each of next 7 sts, join with a Sl st in 3rd ch of beg ch-3. Fasten off. (21 dc across each side, 4 ch-3 sps)

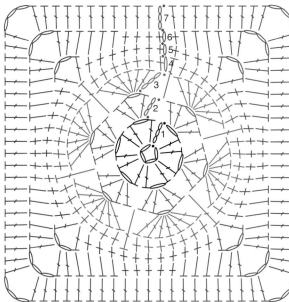

orange cappuccino tote

Paula's Pendant squares were crocheted in rich, coffee-shop colors to create a sophisticated tapestry look. The tote has convenient gusset pockets that appear almost hidden in the surrounding motifs. Sturdy leather handles lend a stylish retro vibe.

Yarn: 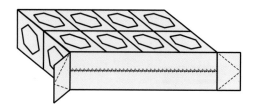 3

Tahki Cotton Classic Lite, 100% mercerized cotton, 146 yd (135 m), 1.75 oz (50 g): 3 skeins each of #4336 Bittersweet Chocolate (A) and #4310 Latte (B), 1 skein each of #4405 Tangerine (C), #4253 Wheat (D), and #4248 Milk Chocolate (E)

Hook: E-4 (3.5 mm)

Notions: ¾ yd (0.7 m) of lining fabric, 6" x 40" (15 x 101.5 cm) strip of heavy-duty interfacing, 1 button and clasp closure or one 1¼" (3.2 cm) button, 1 pair 24" (61 cm) leather handles

Gauge: Each square = 4" x 4" (10 x 10 cm); 22 sts and 26 rows sc = 4" (10 cm)

Finished Size: 16" (40.5 cm) wide x 9" (23 cm) high x 4" (10 cm) deep

Skill Level: Experienced

ASSEMBLY DIAGRAMS

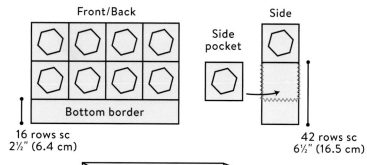

Front/Back

Side pocket

Side

16 rows sc
2½" (6.4 cm)

42 rows sc
6½" (16.5 cm)

Bottom border

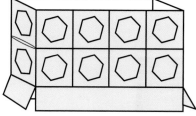

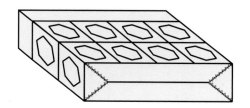

SQUARES

Make 20 Paula's Pendant Squares (page 57) using C for Rnd 1; E for Rnd 2; D for Rnd 3; A for Rnd 4; and B for Rnds 5, 6, and 7.

BACK/FRONT (MAKE 2)

Using whipstitch method, sew 8 squares together into a rectangle, 4 wide by 2 high.

BOTTOM

ROW 1: With RS facing, join A with a Sl st in bottom left-hand corner ch-3 sp, ch 1, *sc in corner ch-3 sp, sc in each dc across, sc in corner ch-3 sp, rep from * across, turn. (88 sc)

ROW 2: Ch 1, sc in each sc, turn.

ROWS 3–16: Rep Row 2. Fasten off A.
Note: Bottom Border should measure 2 ½" (6.5 cm).

(continued)

SIDE GUSSET AND POCKET LINING (MAKE 2)

ROW 1: With RS facing, join A with a Sl st in ch-3 sp at the bottom of one of the rem squares, ch 1, sc in corner ch-3 sp, sc in each dc across, sc in corner ch-3 sp, turn. (22 sc)

ROW 2: Ch 1, sc in each sc, turn.

ROWS 3–42: Rep Row 2. Fasten off A.

Note: Piece should measure 6½" (16.5 cm) from edge of square.

Sew one of the remaining squares on 3 sides on top of the Pocket Lining, aligning top of Pocket square with bottom of side square, leaving top open to form pocket (see Assembly Diagrams).

Line Front and Back with lining fabric.

With RS together, pin Side Gussets with Pockets to Back and Front. Using whipstitch method, sew in place across sides. Turn points at bottom of bag to inside and tack down (see diagram).

Make 3 lining pockets to hold the heavy-duty interfacing (see page 119) for sides and bottom of bag. Side pockets will be 4" (10 cm) x 8" (20.5 cm), bottom pocket will be 4½" (11.5 cm) x 16" (40.5 cm).

Pin the finished pieces to inside of bag on sides and bottom, sew in place.

TOP BORDER

RND 1: With RS facing, join B with a Sl st in corner ch-3 sp at side of square on top of Gusset, ch 3 (counts as dc here and throughout), *dc in each dc across square, dc in the corner ch-3 sp, sk the seam**, dc in next corner ch-3 sp, rep from * around top, ending last rep at **, join with a Sl st in the top of beg ch-3.

RNDS 2–3: Ch 3, dc in each dc around, join with a Sl st in the top of beg ch-3.

RND 4: Ch 1, sc in each dc around, join with a Sl st in first sc. Fasten off.

FINISHING

Sew on handles, sew on button and clasp closure.

ALTERNATIVE BUTTON LOOP

If a button is used alone, make Button Loop as follows: Join 2 strands of B to center st at top Back of bag. With 2 strands held together as one, ch 22, Sl st in same st as joining. Fasten off B.

BAG 17

queen-size carryall

Truly a bag for all seasons, this colorful shoulder carryall is large enough for your stuff. Use it as a project bag, a beach bag, or even a diaper bag. A black background makes the jewel tones pop, and the stylishly linear strap offsets the granny squares for just the right amount of geometrical contrast.

Yarn: (3)

Lion Brand Modern Baby, 50% acrylic, 50% nylon, 173 yd (158 m), 2.6 oz (75 g): 2 skeins each of #158 Yellow (A), #147 Purple (B), #130 Green (C), #102 Pink (D), and #148 Turquoise (E), 3 skeins of #153 Black (F)

Hook: G-6 (4 mm)

Notions: ¾ yd (0.7 m) of lining fabric

Gauge: Each square = 5½" x 5½" (14 x 14 cm)

Finished Size: 18" (45.5 cm) wide x 20" (51 cm) deep, including gusset

Skill Level: Experienced

SQUARES

Make 18 Paula's Pendant Squares (page 57) in the following color sequences:

Square A (make 6): Use A for Rnd 1; C for Rnd 2; B for Rnd 3; F for Rnds 4 and 7; and D for Rnds 5 and 6. Fasten off, leaving a sewing length.

Square B (make 6): Use A for Rnd 1; C for Rnd 2; E for Rnd 3; F for Rnds 4 and 7; and B for Rnds 5 and 6. Fasten off, leaving a sewing length.

Square C (make 6): Use A for Rnd 1; C for Rnd 2; D for Rnd 3; F for Rnds 4 and 7; and E for Rnds 5 and 6. Fasten off, leaving a sewing length.

FRONT/BACK

Arrange squares as shown in Assembly Diagram. Using whipstitch method, sew together from WS.

ASSEMBLY DIAGRAM

A	B	C
B	C	A
C	A	B

(continued)

GUSSET/STRAP

dc3tog: [Yo, pick up a loop in next dc, yo, draw through 2 loops on hook] 3 times, yo, draw through all 4 loops on hook.

Each row will be worked from RS. Yarn is fastened off at end of each row. Next color is joined at the beginning of the row.

With F, ch 348.

ROW 1: Sc in 2nd ch from hook, sc in each ch across row, do not turn. Fasten off F. (347 sc)

ROW 2: With RS facing, join E with a Sl st in first sc, ch 1, sc in each sc across, do not turn. Fasten off E.

ROW 3: With B, rep Row 2.

ROW 4: With RS facing, join D with a Sl st in first st, ch 4 (counts as dc, ch 1), sk next sc, dc in next sc, *ch 1, sk next st, dc in next st, rep from * across, do not turn. Fasten off D. (173 ch-1 sps)

ROW 5: With RS facing, join C with a Sl st in 3rd ch of beg ch-4, ch 1, sc in same st, *sc in next ch-1 sp, sc in next dc, rep from * across, do not turn. Fasten off C.

ROW 6: With RS facing, join A with a Sl st in first st, ch 3, sk next 2 sc, *3 dc in next sc, sk next 3 sc, rep from * across to last 3 sts, sk next 2 sc, dc in last sc, do not turn. Fasten off A. (86 groups of 3 dc; 260 dc)

ROW 7: With RS facing, join A with a Sl st in top of beg ch-3, ch 5 (counts as dc, ch 2), *dc3tog over next 3 sts, ch 3, rep from * across to last 4 sts, dc3tog over next 3 sts, ch 2, dc in last dc, do not turn. Fasten off A. (86 dc3tog)

ROW 8: With RS facing, join C with a Sl st in 3rd ch of beg ch-5, ch 1, sc in first dc, 2 sc in next ch-2 sp, sc in next dc3tog, *3 sc in next ch-3 sp, sc in next dc3tog, rep from * across to last dc3tog, 2 sc in next ch-2 sp, sc in last dc, do not turn. Fasten off C.

ROW 9: With D, rep Row 4. Fasten off D.

ROW 10: With B, rep Row 2. Fasten off B.

ROW 11: With E, rep Row 2. Fasten off E.

ROW 12: With F, rep Row 2. Fasten off F.

FINISHING

Before assembling bag, line Back, Front, and Gusset/Strap.

Sew short ends of Gusset/Strap together. Placing seam at center bottom of bag, pin Front and Back to Gusset/Strap, making sure Gusset is evenly placed on Back and Front. Sew Gusset to Front and Back from RS.

BAG 18

flower power purse

Add a cluster of flowers and dramatic, circular bamboo handles to a simple rectangle of 20 granny squares and you'll have a very special handbag. This vintage-inspired purse gets a modern update with rich colors and pretty details.

Yarn: ⊛ **3**

Cascade Yarns Sunseeker Shade, 50% cotton/50% acrylic, 237 yd (217 m), 3.5 oz (100 g): 3 skeins of #03 Sparkling Grape (A), 2 skeins each of #02 Lavendula (B) and #13 Pool Blue (C)

Hook: F-5 (3.75 mm)

Notions: ¾ yd (0.7 m) of lining fabric, two 10" (25.5 cm) circular bamboo handles

Gauge: Each square = 4" x 4" (10 x 10 cm); 20 sts = 4" (10 cm)

Finished Size: 22" (56 cm) wide x 8 ½" (21.5 cm) deep

Skill Level: Experienced

SQUARES

Make 20 Paula's Pendant Squares (page 57) using B for Rnds 1, 2, and 4; C for Rnd 3; and A for Rnds 5 and 6. Omit Rnd 7 as originally written. Work the following rnd instead:

RND 7: With A, ch 1, *sc in each dc to next corner, (2 sc, ch 3, 2 sc) in corner ch-3 sp, rep from * around, sc in each st to beg, join with a Sl st in first sc. Fasten off, leaving a long sewing length.

Using the whipstitch method, sew squares together in a rectangle, 5 wide by 4 high.

FIRST SIDE EDGING

ROW 1: With RS facing, join A with a Sl st in top left-hand corner ch-3 sp, ch 3 (counts as dc here and throughout), working across side of rectangle, *sk next sc, dc in each of next 19 sc, sk next sc**, dc in each of next 2 ch-3 sps, rep from * across, ending last rep at **, dc in last ch-3 sp, turn. (84 dc)

ROW 2: Ch 3, dc in each dc across, turn. Fasten off, leaving a sewing length.

SECOND SIDE EDGING

Rep First Side Edging on other side of rectangle.

FINISHING

Line bag while flat. Fold rectangle in half lengthwise. Sew side seams from bottom fold across 1 ½ squares, leaving ½ square open at top.

(continued)

TOP BORDER

ROW 1: With RS facing, join A with a Sl st in top right-hand corner, ch 3, *sk next st, dc in next st, rep from * across top edge to next corner ch-3 sp, turn. (60 dc)

ROW 2: Ch 3, *dc2tog over next 2 sts, rep from * across, dc in last st, turn. (31 sts)

ROW 3: Ch 1, sc in first st, *sk next st, sc in next st, rep from * across. Fasten off, leaving a 2 yd (1.8 m) sewing length.

Repeat Top Border on other top edge.

HANDLES

Thread a 2 yd (1.8 m) length of yarn onto a tapestry needle; working around the handle, whipstitch handle to last row of sc. Fasten off securely.

FLOWER EMBELLISHMENT

Make 2 Five-Petal Flowers with B, 1 flower each with A and C. Fasten off, leaving a sewing length.

Make 3 Broad Leaf motifs with C. Fasten off, leaving a sewing length.

Sew Flowers and Leaves to Front of bag as shown in photo.

BROAD LEAF

Note: Work leaf on both sides of the foundation chain.

Ch 14.

First half of leaf: 5 tr in 5th ch from hook, 1 tr in each of the next 3 ch, 1 dc in each of the next 2 ch, 1 hdc in each of the next 2 ch, 1 sc in next ch, 1 Sl st in last ch, ch 3, Sl st in the same ch (point of leaf), do not turn.

Second half of leaf: Working across opposite side of foundation ch, 1 sc in next ch, 1 hdc in each of next 2 ch, 1 dc in each of next 2 ch, 1 tr in each of next 3 ch, 5 tr in last ch, ch 3, Sl st in same ch, end off.

5 PETAL FLOWER

Ch 5, join with a Sl st to form a ring.

RND 1: Ch 1, 10 sc in ring, join with a sl st to first sc.

RND 2: *Ch 2, 5 tr in next sc, ch 2, sl st in next st, rep from * 4 times more, end off.

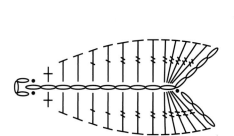

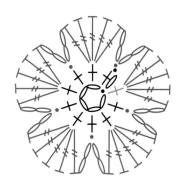

FIREWORKS

Skill Level: Intermediate

Made with 4 colors: A, B, C, and D.

Puff stitch (puff st): [Yo, insert hook in next st, yo, draw yarn through st] 4 times in same st, yo, draw yarn through 9 loops on hook.

Beg cluster: Ch 3, [yo, insert hook in st or sp, yo, draw up a loop, yo, draw through 2 lps] twice in same st or sp, yo, draw through 3 loops on hook.

Cluster: [Yo, insert hook in st or sp, yo, draw up a loop, yo, draw through 2 loops on hook] 3 times in same st or sp, yo, draw through 4 loops on hook.

With A, ch 5, join with a Sl st to form a ring.

RND 1: With A, ch 4 (counts as 1 dc, ch-1), [1 dc, ch 1] 15 times in ring, join with a Sl st in 3rd ch of beg ch-4. Fasten off A. (16 ch-1 sps)

RND 2: With RS facing, join B in any ch-1 sp, ch 3, (puff st, ch 1) in each ch-1 sp around, join with a Sl st in 3rd ch of beg ch-3. Fasten off B.

RND 3: With RS facing, join C in any ch-1 sp, beg cluster in same sp, *(ch 1, cluster) in each of next 3 ch-1 sps, ch 3**, cluster in next ch-1 sp, rep from * twice, rep from * to ** once. Fasten off C. (16 clusters)

RND 4: With RS facing, join D in any ch-3 sp, ch 3, work 2 dc in same sp (half corner made), *3 dc in each of next 3 ch-1 sps**, (3 dc, ch 3, 3 dc) in next ch-3 sp (corner made), rep from * twice, rep from * to ** once, 3 dc in same sp as beg half corner, ch 3, join with a Sl st in 3rd ch of beg ch-3 (completes corner). Fasten off D.

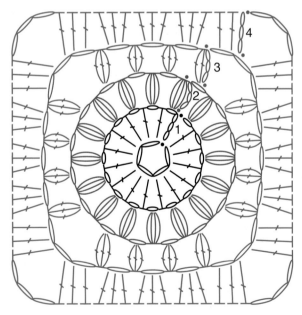

mini shoulder bag

If you like a small bag, just big enough to carry the essentials, you will love this little purse. It's easy to make and there are no color changes: the delightful handpainted yarn does all the work for you. A large button closure in the center adds a simple but stylish design element.

Yarn: 〖3〗
Hampden Hills Alpaca Cree-Ah's Breath, 100% baby alpaca, 200 yd (183 m), 2.8 oz (80 g): 1 hank of Fire

Hooks: F-5 (3.75 mm) and G-6 (4 mm) for Button Loop only

Notions: One 1¾" (4.5 cm) button, ¼ yd (0.25 m) of lining fabric

Gauge: Each square = 3½" x 3½" (9 x 9 cm); 16 sts = 4" 10 cm)

Finished Size: 9" (23 cm) wide x 8½" (21.5 cm) high, including gusset

Skill Level: Intermediate

SQUARES

Make 8 Fireworks Squares (page 70) in same color.

Using whipstitch method, sew 4 squares together, 2 wide by 2 high. Fasten off, leaving a long sewing length.

GUSSET/STRAP

Ch 9.

ROW 1: Sc in 2nd ch from hook, sc in each ch across, turn. (8 sc)

ROW 2: Ch 1, sc in each sc across, turn.

Rep Row 2 until Gusset/Strap measures 50" (127 cm) from beg. Fasten off, leaving a long sewing length.

FINISHING

Line Front, Back, and Gusset/Strap before assembling. Sew short ends of Gusset/Strap together. With seam at center bottom of Back, pin Gusset/Strap to Back. Using whipstitch method, sew in place from RS. Pin Front to Gusset/Strap. Sew in place same as Back.

FRONT TOP EDGING

With RS facing, join yarn with a Sl st in top right corner ch-3 sp of Front, ch 1, sc in same sp, sc in each dc and in each ch-3 sp across top, turn work 90° to work across seam between Front and Gusset, working through double thickness, sc evenly across side, bottom, and other side of Front, join with a Sl st in first sc. Fasten off.

BACK TOP EDGING

Starting at top right-hand corner ch-3 sp of Back, work same as Front Top Edging.

BUTTON LOOP

With larger hook, using 2 strands of yarn held together as one, ch 36, Sl st in seam st at center top of Back, ch 12, sk next 11 ch on ch-36 length, Sl st in next ch, ch 12, sk next 11 ch, Sl st in next ch, ch 12. Fasten off.

Sew button on center Front opposite Button Loop.

not-so-basic black and white

You can never go wrong with black and white. A ruffled flap and a unique, eye-catching button make this bag just right. This bag goes seamlessly from daytime casual to nighttime fancy.

Yarn: ⟨3⟩

Lion Brand Modern Baby, 50% acrylic, 50% nylon, 173 yd (158 m), 2.6 oz (75 g): 4 skeins of #153 Black (A), 1 skein each of #098 Cream (B) and #149 Grey (C)

Hook: G-6 (4 mm)

Notions: ½ yd (0.5 m) of lining fabric, one 2" (5 cm) button

Gauge: Each square = 4" x 4" (10 x 10 cm)

Finished Size: 12" (30.5 cm) wide x 8" (20.5 cm) high

Skill Level: Intermediate

SQUARES

Make 14 Fireworks Squares (page 70) using A for Rnds 1 and 4, B for Rnd 2, and C for Rnd 3. Fasten off, leaving a sewing length.

GUSSET/STRAP

With A, ch 6.

ROW 1: Sc in 2nd ch from hook, sc in each ch across, turn. (5 sc)

ROW 2: Ch 1, sc in each sc across, turn.

Rep Row 2 until Gusset/Strap measures 50" (127 cm) from beg. Fasten off, leaving a long sewing length.

(continued)

FRONT/BACK (MAKE 2)

Sew 6 squares together into a rectangle, 3 wide by 2 high.

FINISHING

Line Back, Front, and Gusset/Strap. Sew short ends of Gusset/Strap together. With seam at center bottom of Back, pin Gusset/Strap to Back. Using whipstitch method, from RS of work, sew in place. Pin Front to Gusset/Strap. Sew in place, same as Back.

FLAP

Sew remaining 2 squares together for flap, leaving a ¾" (2 cm) opening at center bottom of seam to be used for buttonhole. Sew bottom corners together.

RUFFLE

ROW 1: With RS facing, join A with a Sl st in top left-hand corner of Flap, ch 3, work 2 dc in each st and each sp around 2 sides and bottom edge of Flap, turn.

ROW 2: Ch 3, *2 dc in next dc, dc next dc, rep from * across, turn.

ROW 3: Ch 3, *2 dc in next dc, dc in each of next 2 dc, rep from * across. Fasten off, leaving a long sewing length.

Sew straight edge of Flap to top back of bag. Sew button to Front opposite buttonhole.

envelope mini

It takes only three squares to make this darling little envelope bag. Just big enough to hold the essentials, it can be carried alone or tucked into a larger purse. A central button closure blends perfectly into the design, and a twisted cord strap lends textural contrast.

Yarn:  4
Berroco Weekend, 75% acrylic, 25% Peruvian cotton, 205 yd (189 m), 3.5 oz (100 g): 1 hank each #5967 Lilac (A), #5983 Cottage (B), and #5981 Seedling (C)

Hook: G-6 (4 mm)

Notions: ¼ yd (0.25 m) of lining fabric, one ¾" (2 cm) button

Gauge: Each large square = 8" x 8" (20.5 x 20.5 cm)

Skill Level: Intermediate

FRONT/BACK (MAKE 2)

Make 2 Fireworks Squares (page 70) using C for Rnds 1 and 4, B for Rnd 2, and A for Rnd 3. After completing Rnd 4, continue by working 4 more rnds as follows:

RND 5: With RS facing, join C with a Sl st in any corner ch-3 sp, ch 3 (counts as dc), (2 dc, ch 3, 3 dc) in same sp, *sk next dc, dc in each dc across to within 1 st of next corner ch-3 sp, sk next dc**, (3 dc, ch 3, 3 dc) in ch-3 corner, rep from * around, ending last rep at **, join with a Sl st to top of beg ch-3.

RND 6: Sl st to first ch-3 sp, rep Rnd 5.

RNDS 7–8: With A, rep Rnds 5–6. Fasten off, leaving a sewing length.

FLAP

Work same as Large Square through Rnd 6.

RND 7: With RS facing, join A with a Sl st in any corner ch-3 sp, ch 1, *(2 sc, ch 2, 2 sc) in same sp, sc in each dc across to next corner ch-3 sp, rep from * around, join with a Sl st in first sc. Fasten off, leaving a sewing length.

FINISHING

Line 2 Large Squares only. Leave Flap unlined. With RS of Front and Back facing, using whipstitch method, sew 3 sides together from WS. Fold flap in half diagonally, sew half to Back, leaving front half of Flap unjoined.

TWISTED CORD

Cut four 4½ yd (4.1 m) lengths of A. Make a twisted cord as shown on page 120. Pull ends of cord through corner space on Flap. Bring to inside of bag and sew down. Using corner sp at tip of Flap for buttonhole, sew button to Front opposite buttonhole.

POPCORN AND LACE

Skill Level: Intermediate

Beginning cluster (beg cluster): Ch 3, [yo (twice), insert hook in st or sp, yo, draw up a loop, yo, draw through 2 loops, yo, draw through 2 loops] 3 times in same st or sp, yo, draw through 4 loops on hook.

Cluster: [Yo (twice), insert hook in st or sp, yo, draw up a loop, yo, draw through 2 loops, yo, draw through 2 loops] 4 times in same st or sp, yo, draw through 5 loops on hook.

Beginning popcorn (beg pc): Ch 3 (counts as dc), 4 dc in same st or sp, drop loop from hook, insert hook in the 3rd ch of beg ch-3, pick up the dropped loop and draw through.

Popcorn (pc): Work 5 dc in same st or sp, drop loop from hook, insert hook in the first of the 5 dc just made, pick up dropped loop and draw through.

Ch 8, join with a Sl st to form a ring.

RND 1: Beg cluster in ring, *ch 3, 1 cluster in ring, ch 5**, 1 cluster in ring, rep from * twice, rep from * to ** once, join with a Sl st in 3rd ch of beg ch-3. (8 clusters, 4 ch-3 sps, 4 ch-5 sps)

RND 2: Sl st to center of next ch-3 sp, ch 1, 1 sc in same sp, *9 tr in the next ch-5 sp, 1 sc in next ch-3 sp, rep from * around, omit last sc, join with a Sl st in first sc. (4 groups of 9 tr)

RND 3: Beg pc in first sc, *ch 2, sk next 2 tr, 1 dc in next tr, ch 2, sk next tr, (2 dc, ch 3, 2 dc) in next tr, ch 2, sk next tr, 1 dc in next tr, ch 2, sk next 2 tr**, 1 pc in next sc, rep from * twice, rep from * to ** once, join with a Sl st in top of first pc.

RND 4: Ch 3 (counts as dc), *[2 dc in ch-2 sp, 1 dc in next dc] twice, 1 dc in next dc, (2 dc, ch 3, 2 dc) in next ch-3 sp, 1 dc in next dc [1 dc in next dc, 2 dc in ch-2 sp] twice**, 1 dc in next pc, rep from * twice, rep from * to ** once, join with a Sl st in 3rd ch of beg ch-3.

RND 5: Ch 6 (counts as dc, ch 3), 1 dc in same st at base of ch-6, *sk next 2 dc, 1 dc in each of next 3 dc, 1 pc in next dc, 1 dc in each of next 3 dc, (2 dc, ch 3, 2 dc) in next ch-3 sp, 1 dc in each of next 3 dc, 1 pc in next dc, 1 dc in each of next 3 dc, sk next 2 dc**, (1 dc, ch 3, 1 dc) in next dc, rep from * twice, rep from * to ** once, join with a Sl st in 3rd ch of beg ch-6.

RND 6: Sl st to 2nd ch of next ch-3 sp, ch 4 (counts as dc, ch 1), *sk next dc, 1 dc in next dc, [ch 1, sk next st, 1 dc in next st] 4 times, (2 dc, ch 3, 2 dc) in next ch-3 sp, [1 dc in next dc, ch 1, sk next st] 5 times**, 1 dc in 2nd ch of next ch-3 sp, ch 1, rep from * twice, rep from * to ** once, join with a Sl st in 3rd ch of beg ch-4. Fasten off.

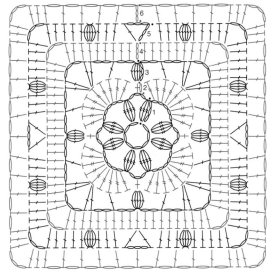

market bag

This bag is perfect for a trip to the farmers' market on a weekend morning. Leaving the bag unlined allows the strong cotton yarn to stretch slightly, so you can fill it with lots of goodies. The wide, lacy strap makes carrying your bounty comfortable and fashionable at the same time.

Yarn: (2)
Aunt Lydia's Crochet Thread Fashion 3, 100% mercerized cotton, 150 yd (137 m), 2.4 0z (68 g): 5 balls of #805 Blue Hawaii

Hook: E-4 (3.5 mm)

Gauge: Each square = 5½" x 5½" (14 x 14 cm)

Finished Size: 15" (38 cm) wide x 16" (40.5 cm) high

Skill Level: Intermediate

SQUARES

Make 13 Popcorn and Lace Squares (page 79) in Blue Hawaii. Fasten off, leaving a sewing length.

SHOULDER STRAP

dc3tog: [Yo, pick up a loop in next dc, yo, draw through 2 loops on hook] 3 times, yo, draw through all 4 loops on hook.

Leaving a sewing length, ch 202.

ROW 1: Dc in 6th ch from hook, *ch 1, sk next ch, dc in next ch, rep from *across, turn. (99 ch-1 sps)

ROW 2: Ch 1, sc in first dc, *sc in next ch-1 sp, sc in next dc, rep from * across, working last sc in 4th ch of beg ch-5, turn. (199 sc)

ROW 3: Ch 3 (counts as dc), sk next 2 sc, 3 dc in next sc, *sk next 3 sc, 3 dc in next sc, rep from * across to last 3 sts, sk next 2 sc, dc in last sc, turn. (49 groups of 3-dc)

ROW 4: Ch 5 (counts as a dc, ch 2), *dc3tog over next 3 sts, ch 3, rep from * across to last 4 sts, dc3tog over next 3 sts, ch 2, dc in last dc, turn. (49 dc3tog)

ROW 5: Ch 1, sc in first dc, 2 sc in next ch-2 sp, sc in next dc3tog, *3 sc in next ch-3 sp, sc in next dc3tog, rep from * across to last dc3tog, 2 sc in next ch-2 sp, sc in 3rd ch of beg ch-5, turn.

ROW 6: Ch 4 (counts as dc, ch 1), sk first 2 sc, dc in next sc, *ch 1, sk next sc, dc in next sc, rep from * across. Fasten off, leaving a sewing length.

(continued)

FINISHING

Using whipstitch method, sew squares together from the WS following Assembly Diagram. Pin each end of Shoulder Strap to top squares on each side. Sew in place.

ASSEMBLY DIAGRAM

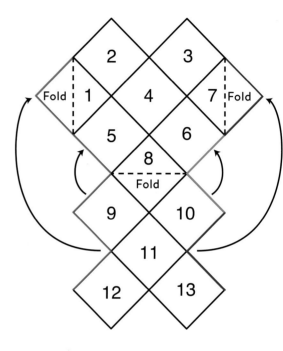

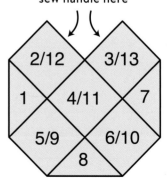

sew handle here

victorian bride's pouch

The Victorian Bride's Pouch would be the perfect "something new" for the bride to carry on her special day. Pearl beads on the ends of the drawstrings and in the center of each square lend a classic, shimmery finish.

Yarn: 🌀4🌀

Tahki Cotton Classic, 100% mercerized cotton, 108 yd (100 m), 1.75 oz (50 g): 2 hanks of #3001 White

Hook: F-5 (3.75 mm)

Notions: ¼ yd (0.25 m) of lining fabric, nine ½" (1.3 cm) pearls (optional)

Gauge: Each square = 6" x 6" (15 x 15 cm)

Finished Size: 10½" (26.5 cm) wide x 12" (30.5 cm) high, including top border

Skill Level: Intermediate

SQUARES

Make 5 Popcorn and Lace Squares (page 79) in White. Fasten off, leaving a sewing length.

Using whipstich method, sew 4 squares together from WS in a strip. Line while flat, then sew ends together to form a tube. Line the 5th square while flat. Insert 5th square into bottom of assembled 4 squares and sew in place from WS.

TOP BORDER

RND 1: Join yarn with a Sl st in seam between any 2 squares on top edge, ch 4 (counts as dc, ch 1), sk next dc, dc in next dc, ch 1, *(dc, ch 1) in each of next 10 ch-1 sps, sk next dc, dc in next dc, ch 1, sk next dc**, (dc, ch 1) in each of next 2 ch-3 sps, rep from * around, ending last rep at **, dc in next ch-3 sp, ch 1, join with a Sl st in 3rd ch of beg ch-4. (56 ch-1 sps)

RND 2: Ch 1, 2 sc in each ch-1 sp around, join with a Sl st in first sc. (112 sc)

RND 3: Ch 5 (counts as dc, ch 2 here and throughout), sk next sc, *dc in next sc, ch 2, sk next sc, rep from * around, join with a Sl st to 3rd ch of beg ch-5. (56 ch-2 sps)

RND 4: Sl st in first ch-2 sp, ch 1, sc in first ch-2 sp, *(3 tr, ch 3, 3 tr) in next sp, sk next sp**, sc in next sp, rep from * around, ending last rep at **, join with a Sl st in first sc. (14 shells)

RND 5: Ch 5 (counts as FPdc, ch 2), *(3 dc, ch 3, 3 dc) in ch-3 sp of next shell, ch 2**, FPdc around the post of next sc, ch 2, rep from * around, ending last rep at **, join with a Sl st in 3rd ch of beg ch-5. (14 shells)

RND 6: Ch 1, *2 sc in next ch-2 sp, sc in each of next 3 dc, 3 sc in next ch-3 sp, sc in each of next 3 dc, 2 dc in next ch-2 sp, rep from * around, join with a Sl st to first sc. Fasten off.

(continued)

DRAWSTRING (MAKE 2)

With 2 strands of thread held together as one, ch 90. Fasten off.

Fold bag so that there is one full square facing front and a half square on each side, mark the sides. Starting and ending at marker on right-hand side, weave one Drawstring in and out of the open spaces in Rnd 1 of Top Border. Starting and ending at marker on left-hand side, weave 2nd Drawstring in and out of the same spaces. When Drawstrings are pulled they close the bag. Sew one pearl in center of each square and at end of each Drawstring.

tasseled arm candy

Make a bold statement with this tote. Combine two contrasting colors, add some flowers and beads, garnish with a couple of tassels, and you have the perfect recipe for a bit of retro-glam whimsy.

Yarn:

Universal Yarn Cotton Supreme DK, 100% cotton, 230 yd (210 m), 3.5 oz (100 g): 4 hanks of #712 Sky Surf (A), 2 hanks of #711 Turquoise (B)

Hook: E-4 (3.5 mm)

Notions: ¾ yd (0.7 m) of main lining fabric, ¼ yd (2.2 m) of contrasting lining fabric for Shoulder Strap, one ¾" (1.3 cm) snap, 5 glass beads (optional)

Gauge: Each square = 6" x 6" (15 x 15 cm); 22 sts and 10 rows dc = 4" (10 cm)

Finished Size: 13½" (34.5 cm) wide x 19" (48.5 cm) high, including gussets and edges

Skill Level: Intermediate

SQUARES

Make 12 Popcorn and Lace Squares (page 79) all in A. Fasten off, leaving a long sewing length.

BACK/FRONT (MAKE 2)

Using whipstitch method, sew 6 squares into a rectangle, 3 wide by 2 high.

GUSSET

Using A, ch 9.

ROW 1: Dc in 3rd ch from hook, dc in each ch across, turn. (8 dc)

ROW 2: Ch 3 (counts as dc here and throughout), dc in each dc across, turn.

Rep Row 2 until Gusset measures 42" (106.5 cm) from beg. Fasten off A.

SHOULDER STRAP

With B, ch 16.

ROW 1: Dc in 3rd ch from hook, dc in each ch across, turn. (15 dc)

ROW 2: Ch 3 (counts as dc here and throughout), dc in each dc across, turn.

Rep Row 2 until Shoulder Strap measures 22" (56 cm) from beg. Fasten off B.

FINISHING

Line Front, Back, and Gusset with main lining fabric. Pin Gusset in place. Using whipstitch method, sew Gusset to Back and Front from the RS.

TOP BORDER

RND 1: With RS facing, join A with a Sl st in top right-hand corner ch-3 sp on Front, ch 3, *sk next dc, dc in next dc, dc in each of next 10 ch-1 sps, sk next dc, dc in next dc, sk next dc, dc in next ch-3 sp**, dc in each of next 2 ch-3 sps*, rep from * to * across to Gusset, ending last rep at **, dc in next ch-3 sp, work 6 dc evenly spaced across top of Gusset, dc in next ch-3 sp, rep from * to * across to next Gusset, ending last rep at **, work 6 dc evenly spaced across top of Gusset, join with a Sl st in top of beg ch-3. (96 dc)

RND 2: Ch 3, dc in each of next 9 dc, dc2tog over next 2 sts, *dc in each of the next 10 dc, dc2tog over next 2 sts, rep from * around, join with a Sl st in top of beg ch-3. Fasten off. (88 dc)

SIDE TAB (MAKE 2)

With A, ch 16.

ROW 1: Dc in 3rd ch from hook, dc in each ch across, turn. (14 dc)

ROW 2: Ch 3, *2 dc in next dc, dc in next dc, rep from * across, turn. (22 dc)

ROW 3: Ch 3, *2 dc in next dc, dc in next dc, rep from * across, 2 dc in top of ch-3, turn. (33 dc)

ROW 4: Ch 1, sc in first dc, *sk next 3 dc, 5 dc in next dc (shell made), sk next 3 dc, sc in next dc, rep from * across, turn. (4 shells)

ROW 5: Ch 4 (counts as dc, ch 1), *5 dc in center dc of next shell, ch 1, dc in next sc**, ch 1, rep from * across, ending last rep at **. Fasten off A.

Fold Tabs in half, mark center, mark center of Gusset, place Tabs on either side of top of bag, matching center of Tab to center of Gusset. Sew Tabs in place.

Line Shoulder Strap with contrasting lining. Sew Shoulder Strap to top of bag, centering ends over Gusset. Sew Shoulder Strap halfway up side Tabs, leaving the 2 shell rows free.

FLOWER (MAKE 3)

With B, make 3 Libelle Dahlia Squares (page 16), working only the first 4 rnds for Flower. Fasten off, leaving a sewing length. Sew one bead in center of each flower if desired.

TASSEL (MAKE 2)

Wrap B around a 4½" (11.5 cm) piece of cardboard 12 times. Wind a piece of yarn under loops at top and tie tightly. Slip the loops off the cardboard. Tie another piece of yarn around the loops ½" (1.3 cm) below the top. Cut the loops at the other end. Thread a bead at top of each tassel if desired.

FINISHING

Sew Flowers and Tassels to bag using photo as a guide.

Cover a ¾" (2 cm) snap with main lining fabric. Sew snap to inside at center top of bag.

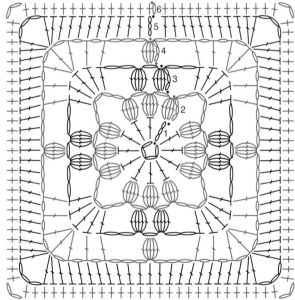

VENETIAN STAR

Skill Level: Intermediate

Beginning popcorn (beg pc): Ch 3 (counts as dc), 4 dc in same st or sp, drop loop from hook, insert hook in the 3rd ch of beg ch-3, pick up the dropped loop and draw through.

Popcorn (pc): Work 5 dc in same st or sp, drop loop from hook, insert hook in the first of the 5 dc just made, pick up dropped loop and draw through.

Ch 4, join with a Sl st to form a ring.

RND 1: Ch 3 (counts as dc here and throughout), 11 dc in ring, join with a Sl st in 3rd ch of beg ch-3. (12 dc)

RND 2: Beg pc in first st, (ch 1, pc) in each of next 2 dc, *ch 5, (1 pc, ch 1) in each of next 2 dc, 1 pc in next dc, rep from * twice, ch 5, join with a Sl st in 3rd ch of beg ch-3.

RND 3: Sl st in next ch-1 sp, beg pc in first sp, ch 1, 1 pc in next ch-1 sp, *ch 2, 5 dc in next ch-5 sp, ch 2**, 1 pc in next ch-1 sp, ch 1, 1 pc in next ch-1 sp, rep from * twice, rep from * to ** once, join with a Sl st in 3rd ch of beg ch-3.

RND 4: Sl st in next ch-1 sp, beg pc in first sp, *ch 3, sk next ch-2 sp, (1 dc, ch 1) in each of next 2 dc, (1 dc, ch 1, 1 dc, ch 1, 1 dc) in next dc, (ch 1, 1 dc) in each of next 2 dc, ch 3, sk next ch-2 sp**, 1 pc in next ch-1 sp, rep from * twice, rep from * to ** once, join with a Sl st in 3rd ch of beg ch-3.

RND 5: Ch 3, *3 dc in next ch-3 sp, [1 dc in next dc, 1 dc in next ch-1 sp] 3 times, (2 dc, ch 3, 2 dc) in next dc (corner), [1 dc in next ch-1 sp, 1 dc in next dc] 3 times, 3 dc in next ch-3 sp**, dc in next pc, rep from * twice, rep from * to ** once, join with Sl st in 3rd ch of beg ch-3.

RND 6: Ch 1, starting in same st, 1 sc in each of next 12 dc, *(2 sc, ch 2, 2 sc) in next ch-3 sp (corner)**, 1 sc in each of next 23 dc, rep from * twice, rep from * to ** once, 1 sc in each of next 11 dc, join with a Sl st in first sc. Fasten off.

lacy linen

This tote combines beauty with plenty of room. Because this square has lots of open spaces, the tote requires an inner lining for firmness and an outer lining for beauty. The loop closure features a stack of unique buttons, and the analogous color scheme is fresh and modern.

Yarn: 🔒3🔒

Louet Euroflax, 100% wet-spun linen, 270 yd (247 m), 3.5 oz (100 g): 2 hanks of #18.2454 Violet (A), 1 skein each of #18.2344 Orchid (B) and #18.2324 Soft Violet (C)

Hook: F-5 (3.75 mm)

Notions: One 2 ¼" (5.5 cm) button, one 1" (2.5 cm) button, ¾ yd (0.7 m) of inner lining, ¾ yd (0.7 m) of outer lining

Gauge: Each square = 6" x 6" (15 x 15 cm)

Finished Size: 18" (45.5 cm) wide x 19" (48.5 cm) high

Skill Level: Intermediate

SQUARES

Make 6 Venetian Star Squares (page 91) in each of A, B, and C.

GUSSET/SHOULDER STRAP

With A, ch 10.

ROW 1: Dc in 4th ch from hook, dc in each ch across, turn. (8 dc)

ROW 2: Ch 3 (counts as dc here and throughout), dc in each dc across, turn.

Rep Row 2 until Gusset measures 96" (244 cm) (54" [137 cm] for 3 sides of bag plus 42" [106.5 cm] for Shoulder Strap). Do not fasten off.

Note: For a shorter Shoulder Strap, omit rows of dc until Strap is desired length.

EDGING

Ch 1, sc evenly around Gusset/Shoulder Strap, working 2 sc in each row-end st on sides. Fasten off, leaving a long sewing length.

BACK/FRONT (MAKE 2)

Sew 9 squares together, using 3 squares of B across top, 3 square of C across center, and 3 squares of A across bottom.

(continued)

LINING

Line Back and Front with inner lining, then outer lining. Line Gusset part of Gusset/Strap with outer lining just on 27" (68.5cm) of each end (just the sections that will be attached to sides and bottom of bag). With inner lining fabric, line the entire Strap.

ASSEMBLY

Sew ends of Gusset together. With RS of Back and Gusset facing, with Gusset seam at center bottom of bag, pin one side of Gusset/Strap in place to Back. Working in back loops only, sew Gusset in place. Sew Gusset to Front in same manner.

BUTTON LOOP

Cut two 2½ yd (2.3 m) lengths of B, fold strands in half. Draw 4 strands through center top of Back of bag and secure. With 4 strands held together as one, ch 30, join with a Sl st in same place on Back of bag. Fasten off.

Layer small button on top of larger button, sew in place in center of middle square on Front.

raspberry attaché

If you need to carry a laptop and paperwork for business every day, this is the perfect bag for you. The sturdy bamboo handles and zippered closure will keep your work secure and you looking fashion-forward and confident.

Yarn: (4)

Lucci Wool/Ray Tape, 50% wool, 15% rayon, 35% cotton, 150 yd (137 m), 3.5 oz (100 g): 7 skeins of #3 Cranberry/Rose

Hook: E-4 (3.5 mm)

Notions: ¾ yd (0.7 m) of silky lining fabric, ¾ yd (0.7 m) of cotton lining fabric, ½ yd (0.5 m) of heavy-duty interfacing, one 20" (51 cm) zipper, 1 pair 16" (40.5 cm) straight bamboo handles

Gauge: Each square = 6" x 6" (15 x 15 cm); 20 sts and 10 rows dc = 4" (10 cm)

Finished Size: 19" (48.5 cm) wide x 15½" (39.5 cm) high, including border and gusset

Skill Level: Intermediate

SQUARES

Make 12 Venetian Star Squares (page 91) with same color.

FRONT/BACK (MAKE 2)

Sew 6 squares together into a rectangle, 3 wide by 2 high, using Whiptstitch method and sewing from the wrong side.

TOP BORDER

dc3tog: [Yo, pick up a loop in next dc, yo, draw through 2 loops on hook] 3 times, yo, draw through all 4 loops on hook.

ROW 1: With RS facing, join yarn with a Sl st in top right-hand corner ch-2 sp, ch 1, *sc in ch-2 sp, sc in each of the next 27 sc, sc in next corner ch-2 sp**, sk seam, rep from * across, ending last rep at **, turn. (87 sc)

ROW 2: Ch 1, sc in each sc across, turn.

ROW 3: Ch 4 (counts as dc, ch 1), sk next dc, *dc in next dc, ch 1, sk next st, rep from * across, ending with dc in last st, turn. (43 ch-1 sps)

ROW 4: Ch 1, sc in first dc, *sc in next ch-1 sp, sc in next dc, rep from * across, turn. (87 sc)

ROW 5: Ch 3 (counts as dc), sk first 3 sc, 3 dc in next sc, *sk next 3 sc, 3 dc in next sc, rep from * across to within last 3 sts, sk next 2 sc, dc in last sc, turn. (21 groups of 3 dc)

ROW 6: Ch 5 (counts as dc, ch 2), *dc3tog over next 3 sts, ch 3, rep from * across to within last 4 sts, dc3tog over next 3 sts, ch 2, dc in top of turning ch, turn. (21 dc3tog)

ROW 7: Ch 1, sc in first dc, 2 sc in next ch-2 sp, sc in next dc3tog, *3 sc in next ch-3 sp, sc in next dc3tog, rep from * across, ending with sc in next ch-1 sp, sc in 3rd ch of beg ch-4. Fasten off. (87 sc)

(continued)

FIRST HANDLE TABS

ROW 1: With RS facing, join yarn with a Sl st in 7th sc from right end of Top Border, ch 3, dc in each of next 12 sc, turn, leaving rem sts unworked.

ROW 2: Ch 3, dc in each dc across, turn.

Rows 3–4: Rep Row 2.

ROW 5: Ch 4 (counts as dc, ch 1), sk first 2 dc, dc in next dc, *ch 1, sk next dc, dc in next dc, rep from * across, turn. (6 ch-1 sps)

ROW 6: Ch 1, sc in first dc, *sc in next ch-1 sp, sc in next dc, rep from * across. Fasten off.

SECOND HANDLE TABS

ROW 1: With RS facing, join yarn with a Sl st in 20th sc from left end of Top Border, ch 3, dc in each of next 12 sc, turn, leaving rem sts unworked.

Complete same as First Handle Tabs.

GUSSET

Ch 7.

ROW 1: Dc in 3rd ch from hook, dc in each ch across, turn. (6 dc)

ROW 2: Ch 3, dc in each dc across, turn.

Rep Row 2 until Gusset measures 56" (142 cm) from beg.

PREPARE ZIPPER

With tapestry needle and yarn, work blanket stitch all around zipper (as shown on page 122).

LINING (MAKE 2)

Cut a piece of silky lining and a piece of cotton lining, ½" (1.3 cm) larger than Back on all sides. With RS of lining pieces together, sew sides and bottom seams, leaving top edge open. Turn RS out, forming a pocket. Cut a piece of heavy-duty interfacing the exact size of the Back, slip the interfacing into the pocket lining, and sew top closed (as shown on page 119). Sew linings onto Back and Front.

Line Gusset with silky lining fabric and cotton lining fabric only.

ASSEMBLY

Pin Gusset in place, starting at Top Border, around bottom and up other side. Using whipstitch method, sew in place from RS. Sew in zipper, leaving a 2 ½" (6.5 cm) overhang on one end. Tuck in other side.

ZIPPER PULL

Cut a 20" (51 cm) length of yarn, pull through zipper tab and bring ends together. Using doubled yarn strand, ch 8. Fasten off. Trim, leaving 1" (2.5 cm) of yarn for fringe.

Attach handles by weaving in and out of ch-1 sps in Row 5 of Handle Tabs.

cell phone minder

Always misplacing your cell phone charger or earphones? This handy little case will hold your phone and its accessories tucked into two little pockets. It's especially great when traveling. The contrasting fabric makes for a nice surprise when opened, and a handy button loop closure keeps your phone securely in place.

Yarn: `3`
Universal Yarn Cotton Supreme DK, 100% cotton, 230 yd (210 m), 3.5 oz (100 g): 1 hank of #715 Apricot

Hook: E-4 (3.5 mm)

Notions: Two ¾" (2 cm) buttons, ¼ yd (0.25 m) of lining fabric, 1" x 7" (2.5 x 18 cm) strip of interfacing

Gauge: Each square = 3½" x 3½" (9 x 9 cm); 20 sts = 4" (10 cm)

Finished Size: 8½" (21.5 cm) wide x 7 ½" (19 cm) high when laid flat

Skill Level: Intermediate

SQUARES

Make 4 Venetian Star Squares (page 91) with Apricot, working through Rnd 4 only. Then work the following:

RND 5: Ch 3 (counts as dc here and throughout), *2 dc in next ch-3 sp, [dc in next dc, dc in next ch-1 sp] twice, sk next dc, (2 dc, ch 1, 2 dc) in next dc (corner), sk next ch-1 sp, [dc in next dc, dc in next ch-1 sp] twice, sk next dc, 2 dc in next ch-3 sp**, dc in next popcorn, rep from * around, ending last rep at **. Fasten off, leaving a sewing length.

FRONT/BACK (MAKE 2)

Sew 2 squares together.

(continued)

FRONT SPINE

With RS facing, join yarn at top left-hand corner of Front.

ROW 1: Ch 3 (counts as dc here and throughout), dc in each next 15 dc, dc in seam st, dc next 15 dc, dc in next ch-1 sp, turn. (33 dc)

ROW 2: Ch 3, dc in each dc across. Fasten off, leaving a sewing length.

BACK SPINE

With RS facing, join yarn at bottom right-hand corner of Back and work same as Front Spine.

Using whipstitch method, sew Front to Back across last row of Spine.

POCKET (MAKE 2)

Ch 21.

ROW 1: Sc in 2nd ch from hook, sc in each ch across, turn. (20 sc)

ROW 2: Ch 1, sc in each sc across, turn.

ROWS 3–16: Rep Row 2. Fasten off, leaving a sewing length.

BORDER AND BUTTON LOOPS

Place a marker at center top of Back top square. Place a marker at seam on left side of Back.

With RS of piece facing, join yarn with a Sl st in seam st on top, ch 1, sc in each st across to marker at center of next square, (Sl st, ch 42, Sl st) in marked st, sc in each st across to next corner, 3 sc in corner ch-1 sp, working across side edge, sc in each st across to marker, (Sl st, ch 36, Sl st) in marked st, *sc in each st across to next corner, 3 sc in next corner ch-1 sp, rep from * twice, sc in each st across to beg, join with a Sl st in first sc.

FINISHING

Sew interfacing across WS of Spine. Cut lining fabric ½" (1.3 cm) larger all around than finished piece. Fold edges ½" (1.3 cm) under all around. Pin to WS of piece and sew in place. Aligning bottom edges of Pockets with bottom edges of Front and Back as pictured, sew Pockets to inside of case. Sew one button to top of Back Pocket. Sew other button to center front of Front. Using a sewing needle and matching sewing thread, form a loop at end of each Button Loop large enough to be used as a buttonhole.

PRETTY POSY

Skill Level: Intermediate

Made with 3 colors: A, B, and C.

With A, ch 8, join with a Sl st to form a ring.

RND 1: With A, ch 3 (counts as dc here and throughout), 1 dc in ring, ch 3, [2 dc, ch 3] 7 times in ring, join with a Sl st in 3rd ch of beg ch-3. Fasten off A. (8 ch-3 sps)

RND 2: With RS facing, join B in any ch-3 sp, *ch 1, 3 tr in sp between next 2 dc, ch 1, Sl st into next ch-3 sp, rep from * 7 times, ending with last Sl st in same ch-3 sp as joining. Fasten off B. (8 groups of 3 tr)

RND 3: With RS facing, working over sts in Rnd 2, join C with a Sl st in any ch-3 sp in Rnd 1, ch 3, 2 dc in same ch-3 sp, *ch 3, Sl st in next ch-3 sp in Rnd 1, ch 3**, 3 dc in next ch-3 sp in Rnd 1, rep from * twice, rep from * to ** once, join with a Sl st in 3rd ch of beg ch-3. Fasten off C. (4 groups of 3 dc, 8 ch-3 sps)

RND 4: With RS facing, join A between the 2nd and 3rd dc in any 3-dc group, ch 3, 2 dc in same sp, 3 dc in each of next 2 ch-3 sps, 3 dc in sp between next 2 dc, ch 3**, 3 dc in between next 2 dc, rep from * twice, rep from * to ** once, join with a Sl st in 3rd ch of beg ch-3. Fasten off A. (4 ch-3 sps)

RND 5: With RS facing, join C in any ch-3 sp, ch 3, (1 dc, ch 3, 2 dc) in same sp (corner made), *1 dc in each of next 12 dc**, (2 dc, ch 3, 2 dc) in next ch-3 sp (corner made), rep from * twice, rep from * to ** once, join with a Sl st in 3rd ch of beg ch-3. Fasten off C. (4 ch-3 sps)

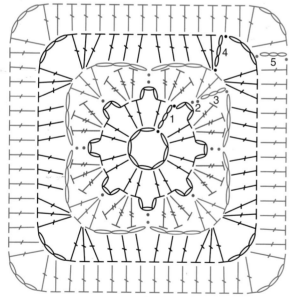

zippered case

Need a little case to store all those pens and pencils, or perhaps your crochet hooks? You can whip this up in no time. The textural motif makes it easy to find when you're rummaging through your bag, and the fancy zipper pull makes the case a cinch to open when you have your hands full.

Yarn:

Red Heart Luster Sheen, 100% acrylic, 307 yd (281 m), 3.5 oz (100 g): 1 skein each of #560 Violet (A), #825 Mid Blue (B), and #620 Lime (C)

Hooks: F-5 (3.75 mm) and I-9 (5.5 mm) for Zipper Pull only

Notions: One 11" (28 cm) zipper, small amount of lining fabric

Gauge: With larger hook, each square = 3¼" x 3¼" (8.5 x 8.5 cm)

Finished Size: 10½" (26.5 cm) wide x 3½" (9 cm) high

Skill Level: Intermediate

SQUARES

Make 6 Pretty Posy Squares (page 104) using A for Rnds 1 and 4; B for Rnd 2; and C for Rnds 3 and 5. Fasten off, leaving a long sewing length.

ASSEMBLY

Sew 3 squares together in a strip for Front and for Back. Set in zipper (page 122). Line Front and Back using desired lining method, and covering edges of zipper tape with lining. With RS of Front and Back together, working in back loops only, sew sides and bottom.

Note: Tack down ends of zipper inside bag.

TOP BORDER

With RS facing, join B with a Sl st in top right-hand corner, ch 1, sc evenly around top, join with a Sl st in first sc.

ZIPPER PULL

Cut one 30" (76 cm) length of each color yarn. Draw all 3 strands through end of zipper, and bring ends together. With 6 strands held together as one, ch 8. Fasten off. Trim ends.

backpack with cell phone holder

Never lose your cell phone in the bottom of your bag again. With its own little case to hold it, anchored in place, all you need do is pull the cord and there it is. The matching bag set is a stunner in the classroom or on a hiking trail, or wherever your backpack takes you.

SQUARES

Make 20 Pretty Posy Squares (page 104) using B for Rnds 1 and 4; C for Rnd 2; and A for Rnds 3 and 5. Fasten off, leaving a sewing length.

Note: 18 squares are for Backpack, 2 squares for Cell Phone Holder.

BACKPACK FRONT/BACK (MAKE 2)

Sew 9 squares together into a square, 3 wide by 3 high. Line with desired lining method. With RS of Front and Back together, working in back loops only, sew side seams.

(continued)

BOTTOM GUSSET

RND 1: With RS facing, join A with a Sl st at seam between 2 squares on bottom edge, ch 1, *sc in each dc and in each ch-3 sp across next 3 squares, sk all seams, place marker in last sc, rep from * across other side, do not join. Work in a spiral, moving markers up as work progresses. (108 sc)

RND 2: Sc in each st around, working sc2tog before and after each marker. (104 sts)

RNDS 3–4: Rep Rnd 2. (96 sc at end of last rnd)

Fasten off, leaving a long sewing length. Sew seam along bottom of Backpack.

TOP BORDER

RND 1: With RS facing, join A with a Sl st in top right-hand side seam, ch 3 (counts as dc here and throughout), dc in each dc and in each ch-3 sp around top edge, sk all seams, join with a Sl st in top of beg ch-3. (108 dc)

RND 2: Ch 3, dc in each dc around, join with a Sl st in top of beg ch-3.

RND 3: Ch 1, sc in each dc around. Fasten off A.

DRAWSTRING

With 2 strands of A held together as one, ch 150. Starting at center Front, weave Drawstring in and out of spaces between dc in Rnd 2 of Top Border. Thread ends of Drawstring through cord pull for fastening.

STRAP (MAKE 2)

With A, ch 7.

ROW 1: Sc in 2nd ch from hook, sc in each ch across, turn. (6 sc)

ROW 2: Ch 1, sc in each sc across, turn.

Rep Row 2 until Strap measures 34" (86.5 cm) from beg. Fasten off, leaving a sewing length.

Line Straps, if desired.

Pin one end of each Strap on either side of center square on bottom of Back. Pin other end of each Strap to corresponding side of center square on top of Back, inside the Top Border. Sew Straps firmly in place.

CELL PHONE HOLDER

With RS together, sew 2 squares together across one side. Line if desired. Sew sides. Turn RS out.

TOP BORDER

RND 1: With RS facing, join A with a Sl st in top RS seam, ch 3 (counts as dc here and throughout), dc in each dc and in each ch-3 sp around, sk all seams, join with a Sl st in top of beg ch-3. (36 dc)

RND 2: Ch 3, dc in each dc around, join with a Sl st in top of beg ch-3.

RNDS 3–5: Rep Rnd 2.

RND 6: Ch 1, sc in each dc around, join with a Sl st in first sc. Fasten off.

DRAWSTRING

With 2 strands of A held together as one, ch 50. Starting at center Front, weave Drawstring in and out of spaces between dcs in Rnd 5 of Top Border. Thread ends of Drawstring through cord pull for fastening.

ANCHORING CHAIN

Join 2 strands of A with a Sl st to one side at top of Cell Phone Holder, with 2 strands held together as one, ch 20, join with a Sl st to top of Backpack to anchor Cell Phone Holder to Backpack.

sparkle amulet

A charming amulet bag does double-duty as an interesting piece of jewelry, especially when you spark up the floral center with an attention-grabbing rhinestone button. This is an easy piece to make in various color combinations to match favorite items in your wardrobe.

Yarn: [4]
Lion Brand LB Collection Crepe Twist, 88% wool, 12% nylon, 112 yd (102 m), 1.75 oz (50 g): 1 skein each of #153 Black (A) and #109 Royal (B)

Hook: F-5 (3.75 mm)

Notions: 1 large snap, small amount of lining fabric, 1 rhinestone button

Gauge: Each square = 3½" x 3½" (9 x 9 cm)

Skill Level: Intermediate

SQUARES

Make 2 Pretty Posy Squares (page 104) using A for Rnds 1, 3, and 5 and B for Rnds 2 and 4. Fasten off, leaving a sewing length.

FINISHING

With RS facing, working in back loops only, sew 2 squares together along one side. Line using desired lining method. With RS of squares together, working in back loops only, sew bottom and remaining side of Front and Back together.

STRAP

Cut three 5 yd (4.6 m) lengths of A. Following directions on page 120, make a twisted cord for Strap. With A, make 2 tassels (page 90). Sew Strap along sides of bag with ends at bottom corners of bag. Attach one tassel to bottom of each end of Strap. Sew snap inside center top. Sew decorative button onto center Front square.

TECHNIQUES

Adjustable Loop

Most granny squares are worked in rounds, beginning with a center ring. This method for making the center ring, sometimes referred to as magic ring or sliding loop, allows you to pull the ring tightly closed.

1. Wrap the yarn clockwise around your index finger twice, leaving a 6" (15.2) tail. Holding the tail between your thumb and middle finger, slide the hook under the wraps and catch the working yarn.

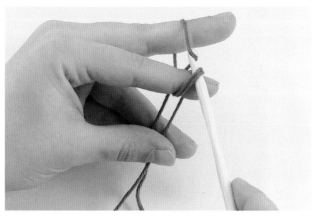

2. Pull the working yarn through the ring, and chain the designated number of stitches.

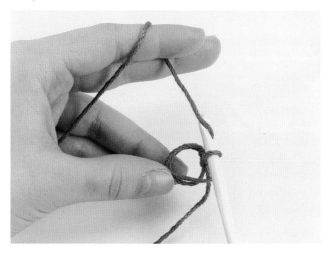

3. Work additional stitches into the two loops of the ring, keeping the tail free. Before joining the round, pull on the tail a little; one loop will tighten slightly. Pull on that loop, which will tighten the other loop.

4. Then pull the tail, which will tighten the remaining loop.

Seams

Once you have crocheted all the granny squares for a project, you join them according to the project directions using one of several methods. For some methods you sew seams with yarn and a tapestry needle. For other methods, you use a crochet hook.

WHIPSTITCH SEAM

The whipstitch seam works best for sewing straight-edged seams. This method creates a little decorative ridge on the right side of the work. Place two squares side by side, wrong sides up, aligning the stitches of the outer round. Insert the needle through the top loops of the corresponding stitches, bring through and around, and repeat.

WEAVE SEAM

I use this join when I want a really flat seam. Hold the pieces to be seamed side by side and, working from the wrong side, insert the needle from front to back, through one loop only, draw through, progress to the next stitch, bring the needle from back to front (not over), and proceed in this manner until the seam is completed. If you draw through the top loop only, a decorative ridge will be left on the right side of the work. If you draw through the bottom loops, the ridge will be on the back of the work.

wrong side   right side

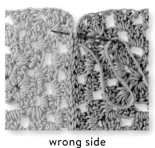

wrong side   right side

SINGLE CROCHET SEAM

The single crochet seam creates a decorative ridge. Holding the pieces wrong sides together, work single crochet through the entire stitch on both motifs.

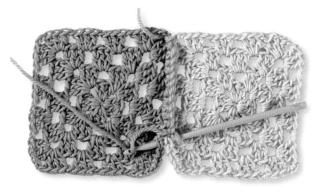

right side

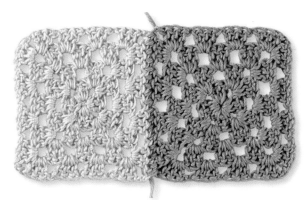

wrong side

Linings

Crocheted bags can lose their shape very quickly. To help them keep their shape, most crocheted bags should be lined, especially those that have open work in the pattern. You do not need a sewing machine; hand sewing is preferred for lining crocheted bags.

I find it easiest to line the pieces before the bag is assembled, and I use a variety of lining methods. Sometimes I use felt as an interfacing and a silky lining over the felt, and sometimes I use a fusible interfacing in different weights, depending on the bag. Fusible interfacing is especially effective for providing firmness to gussets and to support the sides of the bag.

METHOD 1: BASIC

1. Lay the flat pieces on the fabric to be used, and cut the lining fabric at least ½" (1.3 cm) larger all around.

METHOD 1: BASIC (*continued*)

2. Pin in place, folding the ½" (1.3 cm) under, and sew in place.

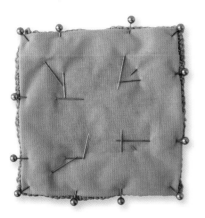

METHOD 2: LIGHT BODY

1. Use felt in the same color as the bag and cut it slightly smaller than the piece to be lined. Stitch it in place.

2. Add lining fabric over the felt, following Method 1.

METHOD 3: LIGHT FIRMNESS

1. Cut the lining, allowing enough fabric all around to cover the piece completely when folded over. Place the interfacing, fusible side down, in the center of the fabric and fuse to the lining.

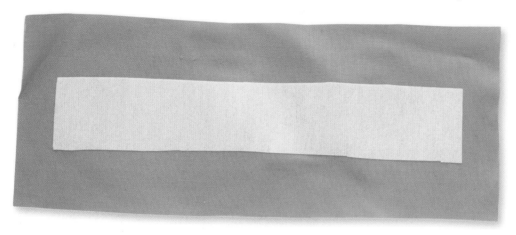

2. Fold the remaining fabric over the interfacing and sew or fuse in place.

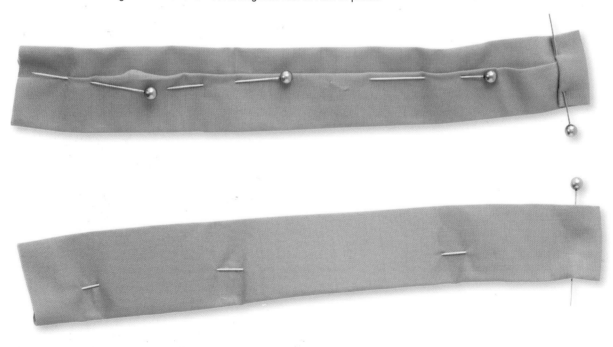

METHOD 4: HEAVY FIRMNESS

1. Cut the interfacing to the size needed. Cut two pieces of the lining fabric ½" (1.3 cm) larger than the interfacing all around, hold with right sides together, and sew three sides, leaving one end open. Turn right side out, and insert the interfacing into the pocket.

2. Turn the edges of the open end to the inside, and sew the lining pocket to the bag piece, closing the opening as you sew.

Handles

There are many options for bag handles, including a wide range of purchased styles. You can also make yarn handles, either by crocheting them or twisting them into a cord. Crocheted handles may need some extra stability, either by lining them (see Method 1, page 116) or encasing a sturdy cord inside them. Yet another option for handles is a string of beads.

TWISTED CORD

1. Cut a number of yarn strands to the length indicated in the project directions (usually about 5 times the desired finished length). Holding these strands together, fold in half and knot the ends together.
2. Pin the knot to a padded, stationary surface. Holding yarns at the fold, twist the strands until they become tightly twisted and begin to crimp.
3. Pinch the twisted yarns at the center and bring the end fold to the knot. Holding the twisted halves next to each other, release the center and allow the halves to twist tightly together. Knot the ends.

ENCASED CORD

1. Crochet the handles following the project directions. Cut cord to the indicated finished length.
2. Roll the handle around the cord. Using yarn and tapestry needle, sew the handle edges together encasing the cord. Catch the cord in the stitches occasionally to prevent the cord from shifting.

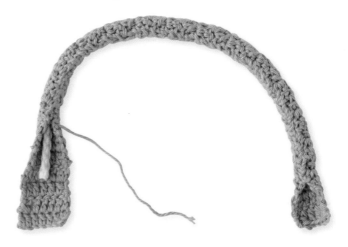

BEAD HANDLES

1. Select strong thread, such as beading silk, and a needle that will fit through the bead holes. Arrange the beads in the desired sequence. Thread the first bead onto your beading silk and tie a knot, securing the first bead; leave a long end for sewing to the bag.

2. String all the beads and end by tying the last bead securely and leaving a long end for sewing to the bag.

3. For extra stability, make two bead strands alike.

CREATIVE CHOICES

With a little imagination, you can find some alternative options for handles at craft stores, hardware stores, or flea markets. Consider interesting necklaces, decorative cord, and chains.

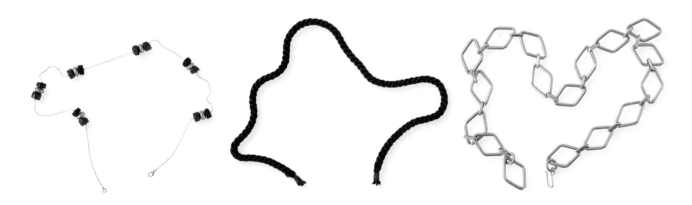

Zippers

You can sew a zipper into a crocheted bag using a hand-sewing needle and thread, and this method is fine if the edges of the zipper will be covered with lining.

1. Baste the edges together with contrasting thread, using weave seam method (page 115).
2. Center zipper face-down over seam on wrong side, and pin in place along both sides.
3. Using matching thread, hand-stitch zipper to bag using running stitches down center of each side, and then whipstitch the edges. By catching only the inner layer of the crochet fabric, the zipper insertion will be nearly invisible from the right side.
4. Remove basting stitches from right side.

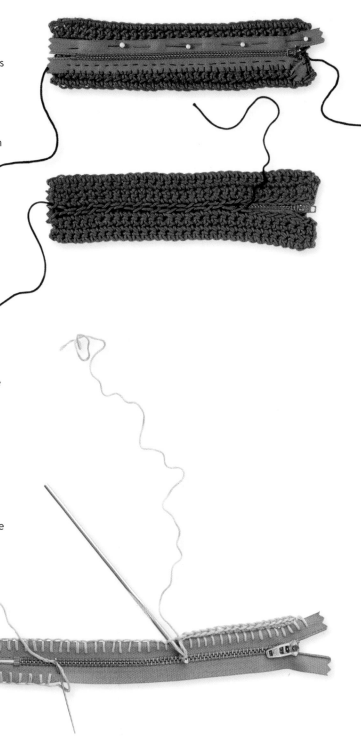

The following method takes a little more preparation, but the end result is sturdier and provides a much neater appearance for exposed zippers.

1. Using the yarn and an embroidery needle, work a blanket stitch all around the outside edge of the zipper.
2. Using your crochet hook, work a single crochet all around the outside edge, crocheting through the outer loops of the blanket stitch. Pin the zipper in place and sew it to the bag using the bag yarn and sewing through the loops of the single crochet.

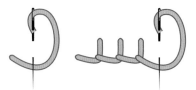

blanket stitch

Covered Snaps

Covering a snap in the lining fabric adds a nice little touch of elegance to your bag. Each snap has two parts and each part must be covered.

1. Cut two circles of a lightweight, firmly woven fabric, about ¼" (6 mm) larger all around than the snap (I used a spool of thread as a template and a fine-point marker to make my circles).
2. Fold the circles in half, then in half again, and cut off the point to make a tiny hole.
3. Using a needle and thread, sew a running stitch all around the edge of the circle. Lay the snaps onto the circles, working the ball end of one side of the snap through the hole. Gather the fabric by pulling the thread tight to enclose the snap in the fabric, secure by going around the fabric again, then knot and fasten off.
4. On the other half of the snap, make sure the tiny hole in the fabric is centered over the indent in the snap before securing the fabric.

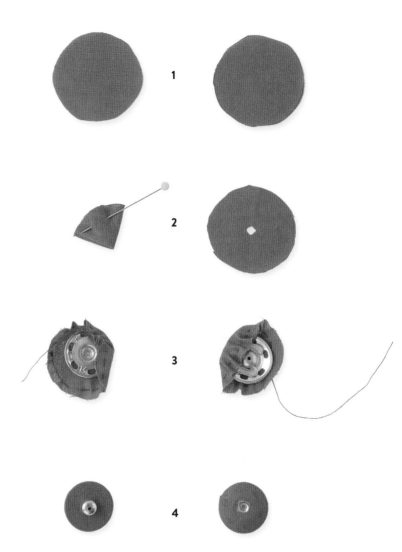

ABBREVIATIONS

Here is the list of standard abbreviations used for crochet.

approx	approximately
beg	begin/beginning
bet	between
BL	back loop(s)
bo	bobble
BP	back post
BPdc	back post double crochet
BPsc	back post single crochet
CC	contrasting color
ch	chain
ch-	refers to chain or space previously made, e.g., ch-1 space
ch lp	chain loop
ch-sp	chain space
CL	cluster(s)
cm	centimeter(s)
cont	continue
dc	double crochet
dc2tog	double crochet 2 stitches together
dec	decrease/decreases/decreasing
dtr	double triple
FL	front loop(s)
foll	follow/follows/following
FP	front post
FPdc	front post double crochet
FPsc	front post single crochet
g	gram(s)
hdc	half double crochet
inc	increase/increases/increasing
lp(s)	loop(s)
Lsc	long single crochet
m	meter(s)
MC	main color
mm	millimeter(s)
oz	ounce(s)

p	picot
patt	pattern
pc	popcorn
pm	place marker
prev	previous
rem	remain/remaining
rep	repeat(s)
rev sc	reverse single crochet
rnd(s)	round(s)
RS	right side(s)
sc	single crochet
sc2tog	single crochet 2 stitches together
sk	skip
Sl st	slip stitch
sp(s)	space(s)
st(s)	stitch(es)
tbl	through back loop(s)
tch	turning chain
tfl	through front loop(s)
tog	together
tr	triple crochet
tr2tog	triple crochet 2 stitches together
WS	wrong side(s)
yd	yard(s)
yo	yarn over
[ ]	Work instructions within brackets as many times as directed
( )	Work instructions within parentheses as many times as directed
*	Repeat instructions following the single asterisk as directed
* *	Repeat instructions between asterisks as many times as directed or repeat from a given set of instructions

DIAGRAM SYMBOLS

◯ = chain (ch)

• = slip st (Sl st)

╀ = single crochet (sc)

┬ = half double crochet (hdc)

┬ = double crochet (dc)

┬ = triple crochet (tr)

┬ = double triple crochet (dtr)

╿ = long single crochet

╤̃ = reverse sc

╿ = front post double crochet (FPdc)

╿ = front post triple crochet (FPtr)

or

⋎ ⋎ = V-st

✕ = crossed tr

⋀ = sc2tog

⋀ = 2-dc cluster

⋀ = 3-dc cluster

◊ = cluster

◈ = puff st, bobble

◊ = tr2tog

◊ = tr3tog

◊ = dtr2tog

◊ = dtr3tog

⟆ = side puff

⎱ = various picots

⌢ = worked in back loop only

⌣ = worked in front loop only

◎ = adjustable ring

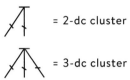

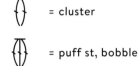

TERM CONVERSIONS

Crochet techniques are the same universally, and everyone uses the same terms. However, U.S. patterns and UK patterns are different because the terms denote different stitches. Here is a conversion chart to explain the differences.

U.S.	UK
single crochet (sc)	double crochet (dc)
half double crochet (hdc)	half triple (htr)
double crochet (dc)	triple (tr)
triple crochet (tr)	double triple (dtr)

quick view
directory

BAG 1

BAG 2

BAG 3

BAG 4

BAG 5

BAG 6

BAG 7

BAG 8

BAG 9

BAG 10

BAG 11

BAG 16

BAG 17

BAG 18

BAG 19

BAG 20

BAG 21

BAG 22

BAG 23

BAG 24

BAG 25

BAG 26

BAG 27

BAG 28

BAG 29

BAG 30

ALSO AVAILABLE

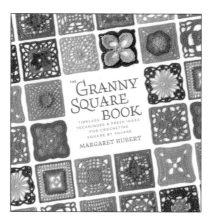

The Granny Square Book
978-1-58923-638-7

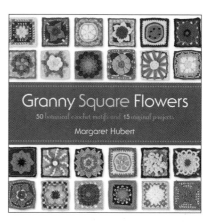

Granny Square Flowers
978-1-58923-780-3

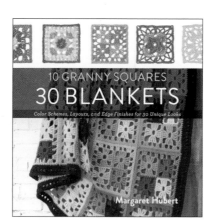

10 Granny Squares 30 Blankets
978-1-58923-893-0

**The Complete Photo Guide
to Crochet, 2nd Edition**
978-1-58923-798-8